SPIRIT LED™

IN THE WHOLE COUNSEL OF GOD

CCAH PRESS

In the memory of Ok Toh the faithful deaconess of prayer, who planted Calvary Chapel Anaheim Hills and is now in Heaven forever.

THE SPIRIT LED™

IN THE WHOLE COUNSEL OF GOD

WAYNE KIM

CCAH PRESS

Calvary Chapel Anaheim Hills (CCAH) Press

CCAH PRESS

PO Box 27693

Anaheim Hills, CA   92809

Acknowledgments and Appreciation

To Brother Alex Kim, Pastor Carl Westurlund, Pastor Gerson Hernandez, and Sister Lily Kim for the continual supports of prayers & labors.

All quotations, except the King James Version of the Bible (KJV), are taken from the New King James Version, © 1982 by Thomas Nelson, Inc. Used by permission. All rights reserved.

The Email address & names of Appendix 1 and the Directors' names & dates of Appendix 2 are intentionally deleted for privacy, while some the Bible verses are intentionally repeated for memory.

ISBN 9780984431878

© Copyright 2010 by Wayne Kim. All rights reserved. No part of this book may be reproduced in any forms or by any means without the prior written permission of the publisher, except for brief quotations in critical articles or reviews.

Library of Congress Control Number: 2010900943

Printed in the United States of America

Dedication to the life time Staff Members – Christian Alcanpara, George Schmittle, Henry GayTan, Jeremy Lepo (Asaph Missions), Joseph Kang, Lucas Moreno, Reza Vafaei, and Seoung Kim (Asaph Missions) - in gratitude for their faithful co-ministries and lovely brother-ship, brought up to our one Master, even Christ, forever, in "Neither be ye called masters: for one is your Master, even Christ" (KJV Matthew 23:10).

CONTENTS

Testimonial Preface	8
I. The Christian	25
II. To the World	28
A. Witness	29
B. Preaching	33
III. The Knowledge of God	45
A. Every Thought	47
B. Why Only the Bible?	164
1. Faith Statement	183
2. Whole Counsel of God	193
IV. The Lord's Prayer	202
V. Personal Questions	205
Appendixes 1 & 2	213
Endnotes	235
Index	239

Testimonial Preface

God had truly worked His miracle of salvation in me upon faith, followed by water baptism on Easter Sunday, when I was a freshman of a College. After becoming a Christian, my vision was progressively changed from my will to His will.

1. My father married my mother before the Korean War but she was barren for long time. Thus, my parents and grandmother had prayed for a new baby at Buddhist Temple for several years. Finally I was born as the first son in a small town of Korea country filled with Buddhism and Confucianism. I naturally grew up in my childhood in spirit of Buddhism, in order to become a Buddha through my good work. I learned Dharma (discussed below) from Buddhist priests and practiced the learning (1) to reach Par-nirvana (nonexistent self state), (2) to restrain my self desire to eat any animal meats-beef, pork, or fish-who might have been reborn due to their previous human lives of disobedience to the Teachings of Buddha, (3) to engage in Buddhism mission works, (4) to do a charity practice to give away rice to homeless people and (5) to do an offering to Buddhist priests. I was elected the President of High School Buddhist Government recognized by other Buddhists. Then, my fear of death and of rebirth to be an animal - especially an ox mostly cursed who provided hard works to farm and to be killed for beef - led me an ascetic life in spirit of Buddhism.

On the other hand, we worshiped our ancestor at an annual death date of grandfather - originated from Confucianism in China 500 years ago – mixed with Buddhism. Only men can worship the ancestors, not women. Worshippers' order was coercive in the order of ages.   My father was the eldest, my eldest uncle, my youngest uncle, me, and my youngest brother. The worship time always was at night. Once I opened an outside door to let the ghost of grandfather come in. Women prepared for food in a kitchen and men brought the foods and put them on the table and finally put the photo of grandfather on the table. Upon my father's order to bow, in order of ages we bowed. When my father asked something, we had to obey him and not talk back. In spirit of Confucianism, we regarded the eldest father in home as the king of dynasty in China. There was a fearful mood to worship a decedent ghost, aggravating my fear of death in spirit of Buddhism.   My strong desire was not to die.

2. During the presidency, I was hungry of truth for why I was born and why I should live, buying philosophical books other than Dharma's teachings and Confucian books.   In a book store, its owner suggested me to read the Bible with my bought philosophical books.   I purchased a version of the Bible there and began to read the Bible by myself through the Scripture in order, while going to the Buddhist Temple.   But I could not understand what most words of God meant.   I went to knock the door of my neighbor, a deacon (now elder), and asked him to explain what the words meant.   He was glad to teach the Bible personally. He taught me everyday.   I discovered the big

difference between Buddhism (Discipline/Punishment and Work) and Christianity (Forgiveness and Grace). Grace is freely given unmerited favor to me. If I committed a sin or failed a required discipline, in Buddhism I could never be forgiven but should be punished to its extent as a result of the sin or the failure. However, in Christianity we could be fully forgiven like snow through our repentance by Jesus name. Also, to become a Buddha, I should have done a lot of good works to people and animals, but to become a Christian, I should just believe in Jesus Christ. For the faith, God imparted the Holy Spirit to me, forgiving my sins and deeming me as a righteous man. I then thought God has the power to forgive sin but Buddha has no power to forgive sin. That's God's power in me, neither my power nor any man's power. I quitted the presidency at the temple and was severely criticized by the members of the temple, especially who had engaged in my Buddhism mission work. And I went to a class of the Bible at the Church where the Deacon went, every Wednesday. One day I prayed by myself and read the Word of God, John 3:16," For God so loved the world that he gave his one and only Son, that whoever believes in him shall not perish but have eternal life," I felt God directly told me about the word which is because of my faith, upon Jesus' death with blood shed as sinner's (my) substitute, I had the good news not to die but to have eternal life, the answer of my strong desire not to die grown from Buddhist's life as the Bible says in Hebrews 2:15, "…release those who through fear of death were all their lifetime subject to bondage." So, I was so excited. Then I by myself confessed my long disobedience to God and repent the disobedience before God by Jesus name. And I invited Jesus Christ to live into my life, as my Savior and Lord. I became a born-again Christian. But I didn't dedicate my time to the church where a deacon went, because I was busy to prepare for a college entrance examination.

3. The interest of animals derived from "rebirth" of Buddhism led me to desire to have Biology major at a college. And Jesus' grace changed me from my burden come from the disciplines required by Buddhism to freedom to eat meat. Later, I as a freshman went to a restaurant with my girlfriend (now my wife) to eat beef. She told me I ate the beef well. The most prestigious Christian college, which American missionaries founded in the first time as a college and a hospital in Korean history, is located in the Capital city, Seoul, Korea. I wished to go there from my home town. However, for my high school score I was hard to go there.   I was counseled by a pastor of the church where I went occasionally. He opened 3 John 1:2, "Beloved, I pray that you may prosper in all things and be in health, just as your soul prospers," and taught me God's promise "to prosper in all things." Upon your faith of the word "to prosper in all things" I was told that I had to pray to God consistently to enter into the Biology major of the college and to study hard (discussed below in "faith movement" and "prosperity gospel."). Accordingly, I slept daily only for 4 hours and I studied the college entrance examination for the left hours. After 6 months, miraculously I was admitted.   It was discovered later that my story was publically announced by an English teacher at the high school, as a

successful story to encourage the students to study hard. Now I think that God's grace prevailed over the pastor's mistaken teaching and my practice.

4. I was admitted into the college and took a course of the Bible for 1 year and went to a church in Seoul, Korea, every Sunday. On Easter Sunday, I got baptized with water by the pastor of the church, after I confessed publicly the creed of Apostles. The church was a Presbyterian local church, which was later discovered as a right wing Calvinistic church by Pastor Duke Kim, who also grew up at a same denominational church in Korea. The church taught us Calvinism and asked us to practice the Calvinism. In the discrepancy between the College Bible teaching and this church teaching, I faced the turmoil of denominations during whole college life. Our emphasis of Calvinism over Armianism's "universal atonement," known as redemption of everybody, developed (1) superior feelings to and (2) looking down the other denominational churches, especially Methodist and Pentecostal churches influenced by Armianism. The long question of whether or not salvation might be lost did not end until Pastor Carl Westerlund brought 2 Corinthians 13:5 in a class, as discussed below. But I got taught "no human free will" at "unconditional election" of Calvinism, because already saved ones are predestined by foreknowing and sovereign God before their birth while unsaved ones are predestined in light of Romans 8:29, "For whom He foreknew, He also predestined *to be* conformed to the image of His Son, that He might be the firstborn among many brethren." If so, how come we preach

Gospel to the World? Each salvation was decided before his birth. The church taught me we should do so because of Jesus' commandment to "go therefore and make disciples... (Matthew 28:19)." A question of human free will bothered me. When we went to a restaurant after service, a waiter came up before us and gave a menu board to us to order. Then, I thought I should choose which one of the foods listed on the menu board. I asked by myself "Is it my free will to choose which food?"   Also the church taught today a gift of tongue was prohibited, causing my fear or weir feeling of tongue speakers. But no clear answer about "free will" and "tongue" was gotten until Pastor Chuck Smith taught the "five points of Calvinism" and the "gifts of the Holy Spirit" in a class (below).

5. In the biology major, I learned Charles Darwin's "On the Origin of Species" and pro-acetate origin of biological organism. 4.7 billion years ago (usually different years by scholars), the pro-acetate is naturally developed to amino acid, protein, cell, plankton, fish, amphibians, reptiles, birds, mammals, and finally men on the earth. I believed evolution as a tool of God's creation, known as "evolutional creation," and ironically taught it later to the students at a college and even at a church, until pastor Chuck Smith taught pure divine creation at church, and repented the compromised teaching (below) .

6. While I was a senior student in the college, a pastor who taught the Bible in my class asked me to help him to plant a local church for a while in Southern area of Seoul, where now is

mostly developed in Korea. I decided to do so. While I was going to the Presbyterian Church every Sunday morning, I ministered there usually every Sunday afternoon for about 3 months. So every Sunday I served two churches, namely, a morning church and an afternoon church. In the afternoon church, I got experienced a sort of a postmodernism culture (acknowledged later). In a communion service at the afternoon church, we used a Korean traditional wine made with rice instead of "grape juice" because the pastor explained Jesus used as "wine" at the historical culture of Israel where Israelites in a hot weather were hard to get a grape juice easily decayed but to have a wine not easily decayed.   To Korean historical culture, equally the Korean traditional wine is the best suitable drink to be the symbol of Jesus' blood shed.   Also, during the Bible study he led us to bring up our thoughts to reach a reasonably understood idea rather than the Bible itself. For example, Gospel Mark would be written earlier than other gospels with various reasons – missed genealogies about Jesus, not in detail writing, or any possible thoughts to liberate doctrines, pre-concepts, or prejudice. The members of the Bible Study, who were mainly college teachers and students, seemed researchers "to deconstruct the meaning of the Bible and to reconstruct the meaning combined with the thoughts of people," rather than pupils to "be perfect, thoroughly finished unto all good works" (2 Timothy 3:17b). On Easter Sunday afternoon, he delivered the sermon about Jesus' resurrection. "We don't know whether or not Jesus was resurrected.   After Jesus' death, His teaching in the hearts of His left 11 disciples was resurrected." But next week on Sunday morning service, my confession of "Apostles' creed," "the third day He rose again from the dead," troubled me much. After the service, I asked seriously a question to a Youth pastor, who answered "really occurred resurrection of Jesus" and why former Christians were martyred because of their faith in the resurrected Jesus, convicting me to trust firmly in His resurrection. No symbolic resurrection! Thereafter, I left the afternoon church. I think I already tasted postmodernism in emerging church or new age movement, as discussed below.

7. In suburbs of Seoul, there were retreat centers, where a pastor usually resided, invited local church members, provided lodge and/or food, prayed, and delivered message, at certain fee. I with my friends at the church climbed up on a mount retreat center and lodged for 5 days. Daily prayer for early morning time (usually 5:30 AM), morning service, afternoon service, and evening service were held beyond eating time. Service time was really long. After delivery of a message, the pastor often asked us to pray loudly. Then, participants spoke loudly to the Lord. Some shook. Some fell down. Some laughed. Most of them spoke tongues, which I got feared and felt weir in influence of the teaching of a prohibited gift. But we got extreme feeling. The pastor walked with prayer of tongue around us and asked each of us for an intercessional prayer. He stood behind me who prayed with a little voice and asked me to pray for tongue. I prayed so. After the next prayer meeting, he asked me again to pray for tongue. After then when he went to me I prayed with a word dropping out consonants before him. Then he walked away

to a next person. In a next service, he announced a patient who was miraculously healed from her chronic back-pain during this morning prayer time and she stood up before us and we raised hands, crying out "Hallelujah, Hallelujah, Hallelujah!." Here I experienced what "signs and wonders movement" was, later discovered (below). Also I discovered what "Christian's devil possession" was. There was too cold in night and I caught a little cold. In the next Morning Prayer time, he prayed for me, "Get out here, a cold devil, in the name of Nazareth Jesus Christ!" I felt weird.   After climbing down home, I felt release of stress with husky voice but deeper hunger and thirst for the Word of God to figure out "together loud prayers with tongue without interpretation" or "Christian's devil possession."

8. When I was a college teacher, I was able to marry a Christian woman, who grew up at Christian home, and so I could naturally bring up my children in Christianity home unlike my childhood of Buddhism. When we got the 2nd son two years after the 1st son's birth, they as infants got baptized at our will (discussed below). Also, my whole family members were able to introduce Christ to my parents who never listened to Gospel nor thought so. They were graciously converted to be faithful Christians, serving now a church.

9. While I as a college teacher taught environmental science, I as a teacher of the Bible taught college students most workbooks (topical teaching) made by the denominational pastors, until I came into the United States to study environmental engineering

and law with my family. As a college teacher, I had deeper hungered and thirsted for knowledge of very good environment as God says after creation "it was VERY good" (Genesis 1:31). On the other hand, I as a teacher of the Bible had deeper thirsted for the Word of God itself to be faithfully understood. However, after I had pursued the engineering and law studies by own efforts for the very good environment at doctorate levels in order to please God, I still felt insufficient knowledge to embrace the very good environment as well as emptiness or powerlessness. Then, my hunger and thirst for the Word of God was mostly deepest, resulting in Paul's confession which is my confession, in Philippians 3:7-9, "...what things were gain to me, these I have counted loss for Christ. [8] Yet indeed I also count all things loss for the excellence of the knowledge of Christ Jesus my Lord, for whom I have suffered the loss of all things, and count them as rubbish, that I may gain Christ [9] and be found in Him, not having my own righteousness, which *is* from the law, but that which *is* through faith in Christ, the righteousness which is from God by faith."   Then, my heart was changed from my burden to please God by own efforts to my freedom of the life led by the Spirit, called as the Spirit led life. As God says in Matthew 5:6, "Blessed *are* those who hunger and thirst for righteousness, For they shall be filled," my life question of the thirst for the Word of God has been filled through Pastor Chuck Smith whose thoughts (discussed below) and life (which I have seen) lessoned me how to understand the Bible faithfully and how to live my life, to the Spirit led life from the life led by myself called as "the self led life."

For example, I had prayed so many times the Lord's Prayer, "For Thine is ….the glory, forever, Amen," as all the other Christians. Also I got taught "all glory to the Lord, forever," not me, as I taught so many times. I saw many buildings at Christian mission colleges and seminaries in many states and in foreign countries. Almost many buildings including even church buildings are named as the names of people who dedicated or contributed somehow, as I understood as they are because I was accustomed to living in that way.   However, what does all glory to the Lord mean? God says in 1 Corinthians 4:7 "For who makes you differ *from another?* And what do you have that you did not receive? Now if you did indeed receive *it,* why do you boast as if you had not received *it?"*   If they receive the buildings from God, why do the named men boast as if they did not receive them?   There are so many buildings at Calvary Chapel Costa Mesa, not any named man who might take God's glory, because God used Chuck Smith as His servant for His glory and so God or God's characteristics alone are named, such as "Logos (the Greek word of the written divine word)," "Karis (the Greek word of grace)," "Word For Today," etc. Donors on any bulletins are not named at all. Chuck is a man with a nature like ours in James 5:17, "Elijah was a man with a nature like ours, and he prayed earnestly…." But he is a man of prayer. Also, he is a servant leader led by the Spirit. After teaching, he left a class room and went down into the first floor. We waited for the next class, but I got a phone from the first floor lobby. My friend wanted to see me now. When I went down to the lobby, I had a glimpse of Chuck's picking up trash on a corner of the lobby. Is he a senior pastor of over 20,000 church members? He is a serving leader who has Christ's mind in Philippians 2:5-8, "Let this mind be in you which was also in Christ Jesus, [6] who, being in the form of God, did not consider it robbery to be equal with God, [7] but made Himself of no reputation, taking the form of a bondservant, *and* coming in the likeness of men. [8] And being found in appearance as a man, He humbled Himself and became obedient to *the point of* death, even the death of the cross." His life, which is total and simple dependence upon God, was an impact on my life (discussed below in his teachings).

I heard of many topical teachings from the Bible at the church where I as a teacher of the Bible served. I got trained in that way. I had noted down every Sunday sermon on my notebooks for over 10 years and once I discovered that about 5 % of the sermons were the Word of God and the other portions were pastor's idea desired mostly for "McChurch," in the book of "The Body"[i] stated by Charles Colson, which is the church drawing a lot of numbers and dollars. We are often spiritually deceived by ourselves that the growth of numbers and dollars is the church growth which God provides, although it is the byproduct of the sermons to keep the people "coming and giving" throughout the commercial business activities far from to teach simple gospel steadfastly throughout fellowship, breaking of bread, and prayers (Acts 2:42, discussed below). I thirsted and hungered for the Word of God seriously. How could I meet Chuck during my life?

10. During the deepest hunger and thirst despairing even of my life, I was led by the Spirit to go to the School of Ministry at Calvary Chapel Costa Mesa, where I read seven books and watched two videos (discussed below, a good impact upon my life) with other books and videos, giving a way to understand the Bible faithfully and to live in the Word of God.   I as a student and assistant pastor had been taught, mentored, and answered by Pastors Carl Westurlund, Chuck Smith, David Hockings, and Duke Kim, who introduced Chuck to me first time in my life.   Since 7 years ago, Calvary Chapel Anaheim Hills (CCAH) has been led by the Holy Spirit, called as "the Spirit led church." I am excited with the Spirit Led Life, newly converted Sheep and with spiritually growing Sheep who are being filled with the whole counsel of God at several facilities and in various languages. I completed all scripture's study and teaching for 4 years. We use King James Version of the Bible or New King James Version, comparing to other versions such as New International Version, American Standard Version, New American Standard Version, etc.   I gave so thanks with tears to the Lord in the memory of converted sisters from Catholics who served faithfully but now are with the Lord, of a converted sister from a Jehovah's witness, of a faithful sister converted from "the Church of Christ, Scientist," of an evangelist converted from a Mormon, of a faithful minister converted from a prisoner, missionaries sent out, etc. Who did so? The Spirit of Christ or the Spirit did so through us. Jesus said, "It is finished" on the cross (John 19:30). Our Lord alone is sufficient. God loves the converted people who become now His children. But He with pure broken heart still loves, not yet

converted people, including recently an occasionally met a Mormon, a Muslim, a Jehovah's Witness, a Messianic Jew, a Seventh-day Adventist, Catholics and a generous atheist (discussed below), "For God so loved the world that he gave his one and only Son..."(John 3:16). Whether or not those thoughts are cast down is discerned at the whole counsel of God, discussed below.

11. In 2009 early year, I got sadly news of pastor Duke Kim, who got strokes and was hospitalized, praying with tears to the Lord to recover him with thanksgiving to the Lord for remembrance of his 1st introducing Chuck. My prayer for recovery was answered so thankfully several months later. While I have been praying in Psalm 71:18 "Now also when *I am* old and grayheaded, O God, do not forsake me, Until I declare Your strength to *this* generation, Your power to everyone *who* is to come," on the last day of 2009 I got another sadly news of pastor Chuck Smith who got two minor strokes and was hospitalized, praying with tears to the Lord to recover him with thanksgiving to the Lord for his teaching's filling in my life thirst. My prayer for his recovery was answered by the Lord through his secretary's email (attached in Appendix 1). A brother who had ministered in a foreign country for 7 years told me about his long hunger for the Word of God, which is the same as my last hunger before meeting Chuck, and encouraged me to write this book of "The Spirit Led^{TM} Life: in The Whole Counsel of God," confirmed with Chuck's message in Genesis at a hospital about Joseph's connective story in God's full control on network TV screen at Twin Peaks Conference

Center, on January 1, 2010. I thank God for His continual works.

The title of "The Spirit Led™ Life: in The Whole Counsel of God" is inspired through my life prayer. "The Spirit Led™ Life" is inspired from Romans 8:14, Proverbs 3:5-6 and Romans 8:28. And "in The Whole Counsel of God" is inspired from Acts 20:27, 2 Timothy 3:16, and Deuteronomy 4:2.

For "The Spirit Led™ Life," Romans 8:14, "For as many as are led by the Spirit of God, these are sons of God" teaches us (Christians) our leader is "the Spirit of God," "the Holy Spirit," or "the Spirit of Christ," excluding any other spirits. The Spirit is leading each Christian's personal flexible life as He pleases.

Proverbs 3:5-6, "Trust in the LORD with all your heart, And lean not on your own understanding; [6] In all your ways acknowledge Him, And He shall direct your paths," teaches us "all" is all. We should trust in our Lord with all our heart. But we should not lean on our own understanding or should not dependent on our own thoughts, speculation, idea, or wisdom. In all our ways of our life, we should acknowledge our Lord at whatever situations, even if we don't understand. And then our Lord will direct our paths of our life.

Romans 8:28, "And we know that all things work together for good to those who love God, to those who are the called according to *His* purpose," teaches us as long as we love our Lord and are called according to the Lord's purpose, neither my purpose nor your purpose, nor any man's purpose, all things including even hardship - not only material prosperity, but also illness, or poverty - work together for good, even if we don't understand now.   These words of God inspired me the front title of "The Spirit Led™ Life."

For "in The Whole Counsel of God," Acts 20:27, "For I have not shunned to declare to you the whole counsel of God," teaches us "whole" is "whole." "Whole" is an absolute term - neither allowing any tiny exception nor needing any defenses - as "all," or "only."   As Paul taught "whole" counsel of God, all Scripture, or the Bible.

2 Timothy 3:16, "All Scripture *is* given by inspiration of God, and *is* profitable for doctrine, for reproof, for correction, for instruction in righteousness," teaches all scripture is inspired by God, which simply means the Word of God, not the Word of man. Here an absolute term of "all" teaches us only the Bible or the Whole Counsel of God or all Scripture provides us doctrine, reproof, correction, instruction in righteousness.

Deuteronomy 4:2, "You shall not add to the word which I command you, nor take from it, that you may keep the commandments of the LORD your God which I command you," teaches that neither addition nor deletion (take from it) is allowed but keeping the commandments of the Lord or the Word of God or the Whole Counsel of God is suggested.

These words of God inspired me the back title of "in The Whole Counsel of God."

This book of "The Spirit Led™ Life: in The Whole Counsel of God" would be beneficial for us who desire to be governed by Our Lord Jesus Christ on the earth until we move in heaven. Chapter one of this book talks about the definition of the Christian stated in the Bible over abused Christian terms. In chapter two, how Christians should be witnesses and do preaching to the World is discussed. In Chapter three, how every thought should be discerned to be accepted or cast down according to the knowledge of God.

Seven books and two videos (read and watched by me during the deepest hunger and thirst despairing even of my life) are discussed with my thought. Cast down thoughts are discussed. Why only the Bible compared with other books are discussed in an apologetic way. In light of literal hermeneutics, the faith statement including Apostles' Creed is discussed. Why the Whole Counsel of God is profitable for us and how we study and/or teach it are discussed. And on going the Bible study websites are introduced for "The Whole Counsel of God." In Chapter Four, the Lord's Prayer as a typical example of our prayers - which are always required for the Spirit Led Life to seek for God's will - is discussed. In Chapter Five, personal questions for us to be interested in a ministry to the Lord and His sheep are given.

Per each chapter, self questions to confront and the Bible verses to meditate are suggested. Appendixes are nothing more than mere references to help ministers for His kingdom. Index composed of frequently raised issues is attached.

I. The Christian

A missionary planted a local church in Japan. He and his wife have been known for long time by our family had pastured the church members for 10 years. His wife occasionally visited in Japan from in California. One young couple diligently participated in a weekly Bible study as well as in every Sunday worship service. They were generous and kind to other members. They were engineers, working well in their company. They often asked sincere questions about the Bible. Before leaving into the US, the missionary invited the young couple to his home. The husband of the young couple confessed by himself that he believed not only in Jesus but also in Buddha and other Japanese gods. His wife also believed so. The missionary was so shocked of that, explaining what the Christian stated in the Bible is to them.

God says in John 14:6, "Jesus said to him, "I am the way, the truth, and the life. No one comes to the Father except through Me," as well as in Acts 4:12, "Nor is there salvation in any other, for there is no other name under heaven given among men by which we must be saved." Only one savor is our Lord Jesus Christ, excluding any other gods. Paul and Barnabas taught the Bible to the people in Antioch for one year and the people became the disciples of Jesus, called as the Christian as stated in Acts 11:26, "And when he[Barnabas] had found him[Paul], he brought him to Antioch. So it was that for a whole year they assembled with the church and taught a great many people. And the disciples were first called Christians in Antioch."

Here, the Christian stated in the Bible is the believer only in the Jesus Christ as his Lord and Savior. He must be the monotheist of Jesus, not a polytheist. We as the Christians can't serve two lords or masters. No other things can be our master or lord rather than Jesus Christ. That's undivided loyalty to Christ, not divided loyalty. Other things can be mammon or money, self, a popular man (often called as an "idol"), children, a car, excitement, knowledge, educational degrees, sex, or whatever. Jesus says in Matthew 6:24 "No one can serve two masters; for either he will hate the one and love the other, or else he will be loyal to the one and despise the other. You cannot serve God and mammon."

After a daily prayer dedication time, a church member came out and asked me to pray for a certain amount of money. I asked why she needed the amount. She answered she wanted to buy a good house. The prayer request itself is nothing wrong. I prayed for her. But several days later after the dedication time, she asked me again to pray for the amount. It was discovered that her strong desire disregarded God's direction, that it might lead herself to become the Lord in stead of Jesus, called as "the self led life." For a while, I by myself prayed silently to the Lord to reveal His word. I told her His word in Ephesians 3:20, "Now to Him who is able to do exceedingly abundantly above all that we ask or think, according to the power that works in us." God might prepare for a much better house above the amount she asked, for His pleasure. God might allow her to get the house another way, not by her payment of the amount, because "God, who at various times and in various ways spoke in time past to the fathers by the prophets (Hebrews 1:1)." Then, I prayed for her to get the house "If God wills" for His pleasure and for her to be obedient to whatever is directed by Him for His kingdom. Thereafter she didn't ask it again. Our master is only the Lord Jesus Christ, who controls my life. My Christian life is led by the Spirit of Christ, the Spirit led life, is not led by myself, the Self led life. Monotheist of Jesus is called the Christian (Christ-like person). When we become the Christian stated in the Bible, the Holy Spirit and the Word of God conforms us in the image of Christ.

---

1. Self Questions to Confront:
   (1) Am I the Christian stated in the Bible? Do I love anything or anyone more than Jesus? If so, how should I do?
   (2) What's difference between the Spirit led life and the Self led life?

2. Verses to Meditate:
   (1) John 4:16, "Jesus said to him, "I am the way, the truth, and the life. No one comes to the Father except through Me."
   (2) Acts 4:12, "Nor is there salvation in any other, for there is no other name under heaven given among men by which we must be saved."

II. To the World

We as the Christians stated in the Bible should live by faith in the Lord as God says through Paul in Galatians 2:20, "I have been crucified with Christ; it is no longer I who live, but Christ lives in me; and the *life* which I now live in the flesh I live by faith in the Son of God, who loved me and gave Himself for me." Upon the faith, the Holy Spirit is given to me. God is working in me. It's God's work, not my work. God's work cannot and will not fail. God has worked in my heart and life, changing me in the image of Christ. In Romans 10:17, "So then faith *comes* by hearing, and hearing by the Word of God," the Greek word of "Word" is REMA (oral word). In 2 Corinthians 3:6, "......not of the letter but of the Spirit; for the letter kills, but the Spirit gives life," the letter kills but the Spirit gives life. So the Holy Spirit is planting a Word (Logos, written word) in the Bible as a Word (Rema, oral word) in the Whole Counsel of God into our heart, and then we can live by faith. The Holy Spirit is never against the Bible.

And so the Word of God asks us as the Christians through the Holy Spirit to be witnesses and to do preaching to the world. Remember the Holy Spirit is a person who has 3 characteristics (1) intelligence, (2) emotion, and (3) will, leading us and working in our hearts, (not self efforts, Discussed below in detail, "who is the Holy Spirit?").

A. Witness

We as witnesses to Jesus are led to live upon empowerment of the Holy Spirit, not other spirits, in the world, not of the world as Jesus says in Acts 1:8, "But you shall receive power when the Holy Spirit has come upon you; and you shall be witnesses to Me in Jerusalem, and in all Judea and Samaria, and to the end of the earth."

A student who studied well in a high school had a lot of friends. He was the Christian stated in the Bible. He tutored language art, calculus, and physics to his friends freely. They wanted to be like him. He was a witness to Jesus before them. Some of them followed him going to church, becoming Christians. He went to a prestigious college and there were many friends with him. He went to a local church and did well like his high school life until Junior. Some friends were becoming Christians because of his witness to the Lord. Thereafter he failed to keep the balance between the school life and the church life since he had labored up to the role of senior pastor. He had no enough time to study in the college, receiving lower grades and even a flunk grade. No any more friends wanted to be Christians but other friends were turning back from the Lord, because they feared to spend too much time in the church to study at college like him. His Christian life was not limited to a local church life but to a campus life and further his whole life. He failed the role of witness to Jesus and the role of the salt and light of the earth as Jesus says in Matthew 5:13-14, "You are the salt of the earth; but if the salt loses its flavor, how shall it be seasoned? It is then good for nothing but to be thrown out and trampled underfoot by men. You are the light of the world. A city that is set on a hill cannot be hidden."

We should love our Lord with the love, which is Agape or divine love or unconditional love, as the fruit of the Holy Spirit. The Agape love comes only from God, why Christianity is not a religion, in which a finite man seeks an infinite god (i.e., from a man to a god, not from God). Without faith in Christ no the Spirit dwells in me. No the Spirit is no the fruit of Agape love. "Love" the English word is described in the Greek Word in 4 types meanings – Agape (divine love or unconditional love), Eros (love conditioned upon opposite genders' relationship), Philia (love conditioned upon brothers' or friends' relationship), and Storge (conditioned upon parents-children's relationship). In those human loves, if a condition is not satisfied, a person easily would fall into selfishness. A parent would rarely take care of other child as her own child, because here no Storge condition (parents-children's relationship) between the parent and the other child is satisfied. However, God without condition gave His only begotten son to all the people for their salvation from eternal death. So, Agape love is unconditional love, not conditioned upon any human relationships, but only from God.

Therefore, the Holy Spirit is leading us to love (Agape) our neighbor unconditionally because of Jesus' great commandment (Jesus' teaching) in Mark 12:30-31 " *And you shall love the LORD your God with all your heart, with all your soul, with all your mind, and with all your strength.'* This *is* the first commandment. And the second, like *it, is* this: *'You shall love your neighbor as yourself.* There is no other commandment greater than these." Because of the Agape love, our God father gave us His son in John 3:16, "For God so loved the world that He gave His only begotten Son, that whoever believes in Him should not perish but have everlasting life." With the love, our Lord Jesus Christ - by His death with blood shed for us and by resurrection - gives the opportunity to be saved to everybody including unbelievers, in 1 John 2:2 "And He Himself is the propitiation for our sins, and not for ours only but also for the whole world." God wants that everybody is saved in 2 Peter 3:9, "The Lord is not slack concerning *His* promise, as some count slackness, but is longsuffering toward us, not willing that any should perish but that all should come to repentance."

With the unconditional love of the 2nd commandment, we as Christians are led to preach Gospel to the unbelievers as Paul taught Timothy in the front phrase of 2 Timothy 4:2 "Preach the word! Be ready in season *and* out of season," extending to teaching in the last phrase of "Convince, rebuke, exhort, with all longsuffering and teaching" and in Matthew 28:19-20, "Go therefore and make disciples of all the nations, baptizing them in the name of the Father and of the Son and of the Holy Spirit, teaching them to observe all things that I have commanded you; and lo, I am with you always, *even* to the end of the age." Amen.

---

1. Self Questions to Confront:

   (1) Can the Holy Spirit work against the Bible?

   (2) What's difference between Christianity and Religion?

   (3) How can I become a witness to Christ?

   (4) What are Christ's great commandments?

2. Verses to Meditate:

   (1) Acts 1:8 "But you shall receive power when the Holy Spirit has

come upon you; and you shall be witnesses to Me in Jerusalem, and in all Judea and Samaria, and to the end of the earth."

(2) Mark 12:30-31 *"And you shall love the LORD your God with all your heart, with all your soul, with all your mind, and with all your strength. This is the first commandment.* [31] *And the second, like it, is this: 'You shall love your neighbor as yourself.'* There is no other commandment greater than these."

(3) 2 Peter 3:9 "The Lord is not slack concerning *His* promise, as some count slackness, but is longsuffering toward us,[a] not willing that any should perish but that all should come to repentance."

(4) 2 Timothy 4:2 "Preach the word! Be ready in season *and* out of season. Convince, rebuke, exhort, with all longsuffering and teaching."

B. Preaching

The goal of preaching is to plant the seed of salvation to the unbelievers, while the purpose of teaching is to water it. Of course, the Spirit leads us to will and to do "preaching and teaching."   To increase is God's work, not our work. Either personal spiritual growth or numbers growth is God's work, as Paul says in 1 Corinthians 3:6-8, "I planted, Apollos watered, but God gave the increase. [7] So then neither he who plants is anything, nor he who waters, but God who gives the increase. [8] Now he who plants and he who waters are one, and each one will receive his own reward according to his own labor." So we as Christians should follow the Spirit's direction in the Whole Counsel of God. The Christian ordained for preaching by the Lord is often called as an evangelist, missionary, or preacher while the Christian for teaching is called as a pastor and/or a teacher.   To preach simply means to introduce Gospel to unbelievers for their salvation as all Christians can do so with the motive of Agape love.

When we'd like to introduce our Lord Jesus Christ to my neighbor or people, first we should pray to the Lord to deliver His word and to open the heart of a hearer before the preaching.   As God says through Peter in 1 Peter 3:15, "But sanctify the Lord God in your hearts, and always *be* ready to *give* a defense to everyone who asks you a reason for the hope that is in you, with meekness and fear," we are ready to preach to everyone.

Accordingly, it is suggested a guideline for preaching of (1) a Parable, (2) a Sin Problem, (3) Resolution, (4) Response and (5) a Prayer.

God says through Paul about the necessity of "preaching" in Romans 10:14 "How then shall they call on Him in whom they have not believed? And how shall they believe in Him of whom they have not heard? And how shall they hear without a preacher?" Also the Lord says about the definition of faith in Romans 10:17, "So then faith *comes* by hearing, and hearing by the Word of God" (intentionally repeated for memory in your heart.). We as Christians should preach Gospel, so that hearers might have faith by hearing of the Word of God for salvation.

1. A Parable

Jesus often used parables in which hearers were interested to explain the secret as Jesus says the purpose of parables in Matthew 13:35,"...*I will open My mouth in parables; I will utter things kept secret from the foundation of the world.*" Here is one example of Jesus' parables of sown seed and explanation to the hearers who lived in and were familiar with an agrarian society. In Luke 8:11-15, Jesus said, "Now the parable is this: The seed is the Word of God. [12] Those by the wayside are the ones who hear; then the devil comes and takes away the word out of their hearts, lest they should believe and be saved. [13] But the ones on the rock *are those* who, when they hear, receive the word with joy; and these have no root, who believe for a while and in time of temptation fall away. [14] Now the ones *that* fell among thorns are those who, when they have heard, go out and are choked with cares, riches, and pleasures of life, and bring no fruit to maturity. [15] But the ones *that* fell on the good ground are those who, having heard the word with a noble and good heart, keep *it* and bear fruit with patience."

For example, a hearer felt deserted from society because of a racial discrimination. We don't know exactly the reason but can see outcome of the hearer. You may bring an open statement, which is a parable, a hypothetical case, a possible short story, or news, similar to his situation or familiar to him. A black American visited in New York City for business. He lodged at an inn, seeing a church on the cross street. On the next day, Sunday, he went there to participate in church service but was disallowed to enter by an usher because of a minority. He was deserted. He came back at his room in the inn and prayed with tears quietly to the Lord. He listened to a still small voice of the Lord in his heart, "I am also not in the church but stand at the door of the church and knock." After the parable, we may deliver the hearer was created in the image of God in Genesis 1:27," So God created man in His *own* image; in the image of God He created him; male and female He created them." God loved him and God wants that through Jesus Christ he has full happy life. God says in John 10:10, "The thief does not come except to steal, and to kill, and to destroy. I have come that they may have life, and that they may have *it* more abundantly." Jesus Christ loves him. God, through Jesus, wants that he lives life to the full, experiencing love, happiness, peace, purpose in life and fulfillment. So, God loved him so much. This would give him a hope or courage from his deserted condition with the Word of God derived from the parable. To him, the Romans 11:12 "For there is no difference between Jew and Greek, for the same Lord over all is rich to all who call upon Him" is encouraging to the racially discriminated and deserted hearer, when God opens his heart.

Also a parable or story itself stated in the Bible could be given to him.

Saul the King initially dedicated to the Lord but later disobeyed Him with 1 Samuel 13:14 "But now your kingdom shall not continue. The LORD has sought for Himself a man after His own heart, and the LORD has commanded him to be commander over His people, because you have not kept what the LORD commanded you." Because Saul's situation might be similar to the disallowing Church who was not after God's word, "the same Lord over all regardless of Jew, Greek, Black, White, Yellow, etc, is rich to all who call upon Him." Saul was controlled by God. We may tell the hearer that God will control the racial discriminator and/or that the hearer might pray for the discriminator to return back to the Lord.

Also you may get parables from "cast down thoughts?" or "other books than the Bible" close to hearers' thoughts, as discussed below.

After a parable, we may bring a Word of God close to the situation of a hearer, led by the Spirit, as follows:

(1) To a proud hearer, James 4:6, "...God resists the proud, But gives grace to the humble" may be given.

(2) To a thirsty hearer, the Samaritan Woman in John 4 as a Biblical story and John 4:14, "but whoever drinks of the water that I shall give him will never thirst. But the water that I shall give him will become in him a fountain of water springing up into everlasting life," may be given. Isaiah 55:1, also, "Ho! Everyone who thirsts, come to the waters; And you who have no money, Come, buy and eat. Yes, come, buy wine and milk without money and without price," may be given.

(3) To a hearer who does not think himself of a sinner because he did a lot of good things as many people say, Adam's story in Genesis 3 (Adam's eating the tree of knowledge of good and evil forbidden by God) and Romans 5:12, "....just as through one man sin entered the world, and death through sin, and thus death spread to all men, because all sinned," may be given.

(4) To a hearer who lacks nothing and is satisfied with the present earthly life, rich young man story in Matthew 19 and James 4:14, "whereas you do not know what *will happen* tomorrow. For what *is* your life? It is even a vapor that appears for a little time and then vanishes away," may be given.

(5) To a hearer who commits a sin but doesn't feel guilty, Isaiah 59:2, "... your iniquities have separated you from your God..." may be given.

2. A Sin Problem

A sin problem to all people including the hearer should be explained with the Agape love as well as its consequence.   We may say that all of us sinned. God says in Romans 3:23 "...all have sinned and fall short of the glory of God." We are sinful or contrary to God's will, being separated from God. We are imperfect but only God is holy and perfect.   Its consequence may be given with God's words. The result of sin is death. God says in Romans 6:23 ".... the wages of sin *is* death..." The separation of sin is spiritual death. The profitless physical life in spiritual death may be told with Matthew 16:26, "....what profit is it to a man if he gains the whole world, and loses his own soul? Or what will a man give in exchange for his soul?"   After our death, we will face eternal judgment. God says in Hebrews 9:27, "...as it is appointed for men to die once, but after this the judgment." After we die, we will face the judgment of eternal spiritual death penalty in Mark 9:43, ".....go to hell, into the fire that shall never be quenched."

When the Spirit leads, you may give any following words:

Psalm 32:1 "Blessed *is he whose* transgression *is* forgiven, *Whose* sin *is* covered."

Jeremiah 2:22 "For though you wash yourself with lye, and use much soap, *Yet* your iniquity is marked before Me,' says the Lord GOD."

Psalm 33:16 "No king *is* saved by the multitude of an army; A mighty man is not delivered by great strength."

John 3:17 "....God did not send His Son into the world to condemn the world, but that the world through Him might be saved."

So we are separated from our God because of our original sin. We need a resolution or remedy of the sin problem.

3. Resolution

How to resolve the sin problem or God's remedy[ii] should be given. Jesus Christ is only answer to this sin problem separated from God. Jesus Christ died on the cross with blood shed for our sins and was buried, and rose again the third day, in order to pay the penalty for our sin - completely reconciling us with God the father.   God loves us and let His sole son, Jesus Christ, die for us on cross with blood shed in Romans 5:8, "…God demonstrates His own love toward us, in that while we were still sinners, Christ died for us."

Jesus' death, resurrection, and justification for the resolution may be brought with God's words:

For Jesus' death or sacrifice, any words of God may be given in John 1:29, "…   Behold! The Lamb of God who takes away the sin of the world!"

Isaiah 53:5, "…He *was* wounded for our transgressions, *He was* bruised for our iniquities; The chastisement for our peace *was* upon Him, And by His stripes we are healed."

Revelations 1:5, "……To Him who loved us and washed us from our sins in His own blood."

1 Peter 2:24, "who Himself bore our sins in His own body on the tree, that we, having died to sins, might live for righteousness—by whose stripes you were healed."

John 19:30, "So when Jesus had received the sour wine, He said, "It is finished!" And bowing His head, He gave up His spirit." Jesus' statement of "It is finished!" indicates His mission to save us was completed or sufficient upon His death, on the cross with blood shed.

For Jesus' resurrection, any words of God may be given in 1 Corinthians 15:3-4, " For I delivered to you first of all that which I also received: that Christ died for our sins according to the Scriptures, and that He was buried, and that He rose again the third day according to the Scriptures"

Romans 4:25, "who was delivered up because of our offenses, and was raised because of our justification."

1 Corinthians 15:17, "And if Christ is not risen, your faith *is* futile; you are still in your sins!" Therefore, no Jesus' resurrection is no salvation because the resurrection was His victory over Satan's power or death (sin's result) power. We must state His resurrection for preaching.

For reconciliation or justification, any following words of God may be given in the Spirit:

2 Corinthians 5:19, " that is, that God was in Christ reconciling the world to Himself, not imputing their trespasses to them, and has committed to us the word of reconciliation."

2 Corinthians 5:21, "For He made Him who knew no sin *to be* sin for us, that we might become the righteousness of God in Him."

1 Peter 3:18, "For Christ also suffered once for sins, the just for the

unjust, that He might bring us to God, being put to death in the flesh but made alive by the Spirit."

Romans 6:23, "For the wages of sin *is* death, but the gift of God *is* eternal life in Christ Jesus our Lord."

John 3:3, "......unless one is born again, he cannot see the kingdom of God."

Therefore, upon Jesus Christ's death with blood shed and His resurrection, Jesus Christ paid the eternal spiritual death penalty for our sins and so Jesus Christ reconciling us with God the father from the separation between us and God due to our sins.   So, God has provided only way of Jesus Christ and we now receive the way.   We should exercise our free will given by God to believe in Jesus Christ as our Lord and savior.

4.   Response

For the way of Jesus Christ, we respond to believe in Him as our Lord and savior in John 3:16, "For God so loved the world that He gave His only begotten Son, that whoever believes in Him should not perish but have everlasting life."

Any following words of God may be given to a hearer in the Spirit:

John 5:24 "Most assuredly, I say to you, he who hears My word and believes in Him who sent Me has everlasting life, and shall not come into judgment, but has passed from death into life."

John 1:12 "But as many as received Him, to them He gave the right to become children of God, to those who believe in His name:"

Acts 16:31 "So they said, "Believe on the Lord Jesus Christ, and you will be saved, you and your household."

2 Corinthians 6:2, "For He says: *"In an acceptable time I have heard you, And in the day of salvation I have helped you."* Behold, now *is* the accepted time; behold, now *is* the day of salvation."

Romans 10:9, "that if you confess with your mouth the Lord Jesus and believe in your heart that God has raised Him from the dead, you will be saved."

5. Prayer

Now you as a missionary, an evangelist, a preacher, and/or a Christian pray with the hearer. Let the hearer simply repeating after your prayer in consequences of (1) admit a sinner, that is, "I am a sinner," (2) Repent sin, that is, "my sin," (3) Believe that Jesus Christ died for me on the cross with blood shed for my sin and was buried, and rose again the third day, and (4) invite Jesus Christ to come in and control my life through the Holy Spirit, that is, "Receive Him as my Lord and savior"

Here is an example. You may ask the hearer, "Let's pray together. Repeat after me" "Dear God! / I confess that I am a sinner/ Now I believe that / Jesus Christ died on the cross with blood shed/ to forgive my sins/ and rose again for my justification./ Please come into my heart/ and live with me forever as my Lord and Savior./ I thank you/ for making me your child. / In Jesus' name I pray. Amen."

I visited on a store where a brother operated and was depressed. After listening to his problems for long time, I was led to give the Bible verses related to the problems by the Spirit in which we prayed together for closing. Then, I advised him a way to introduce Jesus Christ to customers who visited on the store, by simply placing biblical gospel tracts for salvation. The tracts might be available at any biblical local church. At the Book Store of Calvary Chapel Costa Mesa, the tracts are available freely. After several months later, he called me excitingly. A customer who read a placed tract in the store was converted to Christian. Many customers now show their interest in Jesus to him.

Simply introduce our Lord Jesus Christ to the world every chance with an oral or written word and with patience, praying Him to open a hearer's heart and accept Christ, as stated previously in Romans 10:14, "How then shall they call on Him in whom they have not believed? And how shall they believe in Him of whom they have not heard? And how shall they hear without a preacher?" although he will not accept Him if he is not yet ready until He opens his heart.

When sometimes a heretic or cult, a person who believes a gospel different from the Bible, is discovered during conversation, God teaches two ways in the Bible. In the first way, further communication with him is prohibited in 2 John 1:7-10, "For many deceivers have gone out into the world who do not confess Jesus Christ *as* coming in the flesh. This is a deceiver and an antichrist. [8] Look to yourselves, that we do not lose those things we worked for, but *that* we may receive a full reward. [9]

Whoever transgresses and does not abide in the doctrine of Christ does not have God. He who abides in the doctrine of Christ has both the Father and the Son. [10] If anyone comes to you and does not bring this doctrine, do not receive him into your house nor greet him." In the second way, with meekness and holy fear, you may disclose what God says in the Bible to him in 1 Peter 3:14-15 "[14] But even if you should suffer for righteousness' sake, *you are* blessed. *"And do not be afraid of their threats, nor be troubled."*[15] But sanctify the Lord God in your hearts, and always *be* ready to *give* a defense to everyone who asks you a reason for the hope that is in you, with meekness and fear." Through a silent self prayer even during conversation, like Nehemiah 2:4," Then the king said to me, "What do you request?" So I prayed to the God of heaven," you as a Christian may follow the way directed by the Spirit.

We as Christians preach Gospel, i.e., the Word of God for salvation, to unbelievers anytime and anywhere. But we don't worry whether or not they believe Christ because that's God's work.

1.Self Questions to Confront:

  (1) What's the goal of my preaching?

  (2) What is a guideline for preaching? Do I use it today?

  (3) How can I preach to people if I am busy to work?

2.Verses to Meditate:

  (1) 2 Timothy 4:2, "Preach the word! Be ready in season *and* out of season. Convince, rebuke, exhort, with all longsuffering and teaching."

  (2) Romans 10:14 "How then shall they call on Him in whom they have not believed? And how shall they believe in Him of whom they have not heard? And how shall they hear without a preacher?"

III. The Knowledge of God

God says through Paul in 2 Corinthians 10:5, "casting down arguments and every high thing that exalts itself against the knowledge of God, bringing every thought into captivity to the obedience of Christ." We as Christians should subject every thought to understand faithfully the knowledge of God to the obedience of Christ, while every thought against the knowledge of God should be cast down. As God says in Ephesians 6:17, "... the sword of the Spirit, which is the Word of God," through the work of the Spirit should every thought be discerned to be either accepted or cast down according to the Bible or the knowledge of God.   The Bible is a discerner in Hebrews 4:12, "For the Word of God *is* living and powerful, and sharper than any two-edged sword, piercing even to the division of soul and spirit, and of joints and marrow, and is a discerner of the thoughts and intents of the heart." So the Word of God, not our thought or experience, is the standard to discern.   So at the standard of the Bible, the spiritual discernment - containing Agape love and humble heart - is necessary for us to be mature Spiritual Christians, to be set apart from the world (we are in the world, not of the world), to be one body in Christ, and to prevent spiritual blindness.   But we should avoid the carnal judgment, containing critic, hatred, jealousy, or arrogance. It could divide, discourage, or destroy us as one body of Christ. Jesus says in Matthew 7:1-3, "Judge not, that you be not judged. [2] For with what judgment you judge, you will be judged; and with the measure you use, it will be measured back to you. [3] And why do you look at the speck in your brother's eye, but do not consider the plank in your own eye?" and also God says in James 4:11, "Do not speak evil of one another, brethren. He who speaks evil of a brother and judges his brother, speaks evil of the law and judges the law. But if you judge the law, you are not a doer of the law but a judge," and Matthew 5:22, "But I say to you that whoever is angry with his brother without a cause shall be in danger of the judgment. And whoever says to his brother, 'Raca!' shall be in danger of the council. But whoever says, 'You fool!' shall be in danger of hell fire."

Therefore, spiritual discernment is encouraged while carnal judgment is discouraged.

---

1. Self Question to Confront:

What's difference between the spiritual discernment and the carnal judgment?

2. Verses to Meditate:

(1) Ephesians 6:17 "And take the helmet of salvation, and the sword of the Spirit, which is the Word of God"

(2) James 4:11 "Do not speak evil of one another, brethren. He who speaks evil of a brother and judges his brother, speaks evil of the law and judges the law. But if you judge the law, you are not a doer of the law but a judge."

A. Every Thought

Every human thought is not important rather than the Knowledge of God. But we use every human thought as a mere tool to understand His knowledge faithfully. Chuck's thoughts are an impact on me to understand the knowledge of God faithfully and to be equipped with the Whole Counsel of God to become a pastor and teacher. The 7 books and 2 videos I got taught at the School of Ministry for 2 years are summarized below. You may get those at http://www.twft.com/ or http://www.amazon.com/ or any convenient bookstore and read them thoroughly. The thoughts of books, videos, or lectures to make us understand faithfully the knowledge of God and casted out thoughts against the knowledge of God are brought with my thought followed by self questions to confront and the Bible verses to meditate.

(1) Living Water by Chuck Smith[iii]

The "living water" written by Chuck Smith says that Jesus promised disciples that He would not leave them as orphans, but that He would pray to the Father who would send them another Comforter who would come alongside to help them and would abide with them forever (John 14:16-18). Also He promised that the Holy Spirit teach them all things and bring to their remembrance all the things that He had commended them (John 15:26).

The Holy Spirit is to conform you into the image of Jesus Christ. He is to come alongside of us to help us in our walk. He is to teach us all things.

He is to give us an understanding of spiritual things. He is to give us the power to be a witness of Jesus Christ. There is a vast difference being filled with the Holy Spirit and having the Holy Spirit flow forth out of our life like a torrent of living water. The book leads us step by step into twenty five (25) chapters and one epilogue under the four (4) parts as follows:

Part One – Who is the Holy Spirit?

1.   Personality Plus

In John 14:16-18, the promise given to us is "another helper, the spirit of truth." The Holy Spirit is God's special agent, indeed a person, has 3 characteristics (intelligence, emotion, and will). The Holy Spirit acts as person, "speaks" (Acts 13:12, "Then the proconsul believed, when he saw what had been done, being astonished at the teaching of the Lord"; 1 Timothy 4:1, "Now the Spirit expressly says that in latter times some will depart from the faith, giving heed to deceiving spirits and doctrines of demons"; Revelation 2:7, "He who has an ear, let him hear what the Spirit says to the churches. To him who overcomes I will give to eat from the tree of life, which is in the midst of the Paradise of God."'), "intercedes" (Romans 8:26, "Likewise the Spirit also helps in our weaknesses. For we do not know what we should pray for as we ought, but the Spirit Himself makes intercession for us with groanings which cannot be uttered"), "teaches" (John 14:26, "But the Helper, the Holy Spirit, whom the Father will send in My name, He will teach you all things, and bring to your remembrance all things that I said to you"), "Communes with us" (2 Corinthians 13:14, "The grace of the Lord Jesus

Christ, and the love of God, and the communion of the Holy Spirit *be* with you all. Amen"), "strives with men" (Genesis 6:3, "And the LORD said, "My Spirit shall not strive with man forever, for he *is* indeed flesh; yet his days shall be one hundred and twenty years"), "works miracles" (Romans 15:19, "in mighty signs and wonders, by the power of the Spirit of God, so that from Jerusalem and round about to Illyricum I have fully preached the gospel of Christ"), and "guides us" (Acts 16:6-7, "Now when they had gone through Phrygia and the region of Galatia, they were forbidden by the Holy Spirit to preach the word in Asia. [7] After they had come to Mysia, they tried to go into Bithynia, but the Spirit did not permit them"). We can enjoy the love relationship with God, through the Holy Spirit who is a Person. When we seek the Holy Spirit, our goal should never be what we are to look for but to want more of God, and for Him to have more of us.

2. <u>The Mystery of the Three in One</u>

According to the scriptures, God is manifested in the Trinity – the Father, the Son, and the Holy Spirit. If we deny the Trinity, then we must deny the deity of Jesus Christ and the personality of the Holy Spirit. In the Old Testament, the Holy Spirit is mentioned under 80 times in the name of "the Spirit of the Lord," "the Spirit of God," or "the Holy Spirit." In Genesis 1:1, "In the beginning God created the heavens and the earth," the Hebrew word, Elohim, is used as a plural form (the singular is El). And in Genesis 1:26, "Then God said, "Let Us make man in Our image, according to Our likeness; let them have dominion over the fish of the sea, over the birds of the air, and over the cattle, over all the earth and over every creeping thing that creeps on the earth,"" the word of "us" is used as plural pronoun. The Holy Spirit is every bit as divine as the Father and the son coequally. He is eternal (Hebrews 9:14, "eternal spirit"), omnipresent (Psalms 139:7-10, "The Spirit of God is everywhere present"), omniscient (1 Corinthians 2:10-11, "no one knows the things of God except the Spirit of God"), and omnipotent (Luke 1:35, "the power of the Highest"). God speaks in the Spirit's voice. He comes alongside of us to help us in our Christian walk.

Part Two – What Does the Holy Spirit Do?

3. At Work in the World

Three tasks of the Holy Spirit in the world are to reprove the world of sin, to reprove the world of righteousness, and to reprove the world of judgment (John 16:7-11," Nevertheless I tell you the truth. It is to your advantage that I go away; for if I do not go away, the Helper will not come to you; but if I depart, I will send Him to you. [8] And when He has come, He will convict the world of sin, and of righteousness, and of judgment: [9] of sin, because they do not believe in Me; [10] of righteousness, because I go to My Father and you see Me no more; [11] of judgment, because the ruler of this world is judged."). The Holy Spirit is blasphemed by our refusal to believe in Jesus Christ as the Son of God who bore the sins of the world (1 John 5:10-12, "He who believes in the Son of God has the witness in himself; he who does not believe God has made Him a liar, because he has not believed the testimony that God has given of His Son. [11] And this is the testimony: that God has given us eternal life, and this life is in His Son. [12] He who has the Son has life; he who does not have the Son of God does not have life."). We can avoid committing this sin by true confession that Jesus is Lord, manifested by submission to Jesus Christ and His Lordship. Sin is doing the wrong thing, missing the mark, while "righteousness" is doing the right thing, hitting the mark. The God's standard for righteousness is our acceptance of the Spirit's witness about Christ and we can meet that standard only by faith in Jesus Christ, manifested (deed) by submission to Jesus Christ. In Colossians 2:13-15, "And you, being dead in your trespasses and the uncircumcision of your flesh, He has made alive together with Him, having forgiven you all trespasses, [14] having wiped out the handwriting of requirements that was against us, which was contrary to us. And He has taken it out of the way, having nailed it to the cross. [15] Having disarmed principalities and powers, He made a public spectacle of them, triumphing over them in it, "on the cross Jesus Christ defeated those principalities and powers of darkness (Power of Satan) which were against us. The resurrection was the proof of His victory.

4. Keeping the Lid On

The Holy Spirit is restraining evil in our world until the time set by the Father (2 Thessalonians 2:3-7, "Let no one deceive you by any means; for *that Day will not come* unless the falling away comes first, and the man of sin is revealed, the son of perdition, [4] who opposes and exalts himself above all that is called God or that is worshiped, so that he sits as God in the temple of God, showing himself that he is God. [5] Do you not remember that when I was still with you I told you these things? [6] And now you know what is restraining, that he may be revealed in his own time. [7] For the mystery of lawlessness is already at work; only He who now restrains *will do so* until He is taken out of the way."). We find ourselves to face the conflict in the world because we as Christians are redeemed but live in a world under the power of Satan. By compromise with the world, we have been weakened. We should be "salt" in the world, to be purifying influence on the world until the rapture. The strategy of Satan is to bring all of the governments of the earth under the control of one man. His purpose is to create one world government with his own representative at its head. God will hinder the work of the Antichrist, a violent enemy of God. The Antichrist shall prosper till the Great Tribulation period has been accomplished. In this conflict between Satan's power and the Holy Spirit's power we are in, we need only spiritual weapons that have that bring any real force to this conflict, i.e., the work of the Holy Spirit. By the work of the Holy Spirit in our lives, we can be the purifying influence on people in the world, bearing a faithful testimony to the truth. We can expect to be filled with the Holy Spirit until the day the Holy Spirit is removed from the earth, the redemption from the power of sin through Jesus Christ, the seal with the Holy Spirit, and the empowerment by the Spirit to live in obedience to the Lord Jesus Christ.

5. The Church's Divine Helper

The direction of the Holy Spirit causes a church to succeed and function correctly. In Acts 11:1-10, "Now the apostles and brethren who were in Judea heard that the Gentiles had also received the Word of God. [2] And when Peter came up to Jerusalem, those of the circumcision contended with him, [3] saying, "You went in to uncircumcised men and ate with them!" [4] But Peter explained *it* to them in order from the beginning, saying: [5] "I was in the city of Joppa praying; and in a trance I saw a vision, an object descending like a great sheet, let down from heaven by four corners; and it came to me. [6] When I observed it intently and considered, I saw four-footed animals of the earth, wild beasts, creeping things, and birds of the air. [7] And I heard a voice saying to me, 'Rise, Peter; kill and eat.' [8] But I said, 'Not so, Lord! For nothing common or unclean has at any time entered my mouth.' [9] But the voice answered me again from heaven, 'What God has cleansed you must not call common.' [10] Now this was done three times, and all were drawn up again into heaven," Peter got vision from God, "Rise, Peter; Kill and eat," all kinds of animals including unclean animals that Jews were prohibited to eat. But under the direction of the Holy Spirit, Peter preached Christ to Cornelius and his friends.   The Holy Spirit today leads us not only supernaturally but also many times naturally circumstances to lead us.   In Acts 5:1-11, "But a certain man named Ananias, with Sapphira his wife, sold a possession. [2] And he kept back *part* of the proceeds, his wife also being aware *of it,* and brought a certain part and laid *it* at the apostles' feet. [3] But Peter said, "Ananias, why has Satan filled your heart to lie to the Holy Spirit and keep back *part* of the price of the land for yourself? [4] While it remained, was it not your own? And after it was sold, was it not in your own control? Why have you conceived this thing in your heart? You have not lied to men but to God." [5] Then Ananias, hearing these words, fell down and breathed his last. So great fear came upon all those who heard these things. [6] And the young men arose and wrapped him up, carried *him* out, and buried *him.* [7] Now it was about three hours later when his wife came in, not knowing what had happened. [8] And Peter answered her, "Tell me whether you sold the land for so much?" She said, "Yes, for so much." [9] Then Peter said to her, "How is it that you have agreed together to test the Spirit of the Lord? Look, the feet of those who have buried your husband *are* at the door, and they will carry you out." [10] Then immediately she fell down at his feet and breathed her last. And the young men came in and found her dead, and carrying *her* out, buried *her* by her husband. [11] So great fear came upon all the church and upon all who heard these things," Anania and Sapphira lied by pretending that they had brought all of money in order to impress other people – hypocrisy (the curse of church), while in Acts 4:32-37, "Now the multitude of those who believed were of one heart and one soul; neither did anyone say that any of the things he possessed was his own, but they had all things in common. [33] And with great power the apostles gave witness to the resurrection of the Lord Jesus. And great grace was upon them all. [34] Nor was there anyone among them who lacked; for all who were possessors of lands or houses sold them, and brought the proceeds of the things that were sold, [35] and laid *them* at the apostles' feet; and they distributed to each as anyone had need. [36] And Joses, who was also named Barnabas by the apostles (which is translated Son of Encouragement), a Levite of the country of Cyprus, [37] having land, sold *it,* and brought the money and laid *it* at the apostles' feet," everyone held all things in common with one heart and one soul. The tragic mistake of the modern church is independence from the Holy Spirit. We can ask Him to give us His wisdom and guidance and direction in "every decision" regarding the church's function, operation, leadership, expenditures, and outreach.

6. <u>The Manifold Grace of God</u>

The believer belongs to God. That is His seal on his life, to prove His ownership to him. The Holy Spirit is the "guarantee or earnest" of our inheritance when God has given us the deposit of the Holy Spirit on the future glory God has promised us. In 1 John 2:27, "But the anointing which you have received from Him abides in you, and you do not need that anyone teach you; but as the same anointing teaches you concerning all things, and is true, and is not a lie, and just as it has taught you, you will abide in Him," as we read the Bible and ask the Holy Spirit to teach and instruct our hearts, He will lead us into all truth. The purpose of prayer is that we open our hearts to allow God to do the things He wants to do. The cycle of true prayer is that God puts His desire in our hearts, and then we express it back to Him in prayer. We as believers can be witnesses to the world today through the words of believers, through living the life of Jesus Christ before people, and through deeds wrought by the Holy Spirit in the lines of believers. The primary work of the Spirit is to conform us into the image of Christ, and the key of the work is to let the Holy Spirit do in our lives.

Part Three – What Are the Gifts of the Spirit?

7.   Unity in Diversity

In 1 Corinthians 12, Paul lists nine spiritual gifts in verses 8 through 10, "for to one is given the word of wisdom through the Spirit, to another the word of knowledge through the same Spirit, [9] to another faith by the same Spirit, to another gifts of healings by the same Spirit, [10] to another the working of miracles, to another prophecy, to another discerning of spirits, to another *different* kinds of tongues, to another the interpretation of tongues." The gifts can be divided into 3 sections – power, faith, and utterances.   The important principle concerning the gifts of the Spirit is that the true gifts will be manifested in a scriptural and correct way and will focus people's hearts on Jesus Christ. The word of "diversities of gifts" means that the 9 different gifts complement each other and they do not compete with each other. The word of "differences of ministries" in 1 Corinthians 12:5, "There are differences of ministries, but the same Lord," means that the same Lord directs all different ministries – apostle, prophet, pastor-teacher, government, helps, etc. The word of "diversities of operations" means that the Spirit works differently in our lives according to our own unique personalities and idiosyncrasies. It is wrong for us to judge others in the way they may worship the Lord because we are worshipping the same Lord in various ways but in our judgment Satan might attack us. In Luke 11:13, "If you then, being evil, know how to give good gifts to your children, how much more will *your* heavenly Father give the Holy Spirit to those who ask Him!"" God's promise, which good gifts are given to us who ask Him, is given to us, so that we can apply this to our lives just by deferring to Him and to the Holy Spirit to give us those gifts that can best be exercised for the benefit of the whole church.

8.   The Word of Wisdom

Knowledge is the accumulation of fact, but wisdom is the proper application of the fact. The knowledge without wisdom is dangerous because through knowledge we have been able to create super weapons with the capacity to destroy mankind. We need the word of wisdom anointed by the Holy Spirit, when critical issues arise and important decision must be made. The gift of wisdom is more than "wisdom in general" because there are times when the Spirit directly gives us the right word. The Spirit manifested the gift of the word of wisdom where in 1 Kings 3:16-28, "Take your sword and cut the child in two; then give them each half," Solomon was able to resolve the issue of "whose baby." Also in Luke 20:22-26, "Then render to Caesar the things that are Caesar's, and give to God the things that are God's," Jesus blew up the Pharisees' trapping question. We can recognize the word of wisdom, given by the Spirit of God, operating in our lives, as it is so right and so on target, although it is something that we had not learned or studied or thought about. The gifts of the Spirit operate so naturally. It is important for us to ask for the gift of the word of wisdom because the lack of the gift of wisdom often leads division within the Church.

9. How Did He Know That?

The gift of the word of knowledge is a divine gift of knowledge concerning a person or situation that could not come though natural thought processes. The gift of knowledge operated in the life of Jesus – John 1:45-51, "Philip found Nathanael and said to him, "We have found Him of whom Moses in the law, and also the prophets, wrote—Jesus of Nazareth, the son of Joseph." [46] And Nathanael said to him, "Can anything good come out of Nazareth?" Philip said to him, "Come and see." [47] Jesus saw Nathanael coming toward Him, and said of him, "Behold, an Israelite indeed, in whom is no deceit!" [48] Nathanael said to Him, "How do You know me?" Jesus answered and said to him, "Before Philip called you, when you were under the fig tree, I saw you." [49] Nathanael answered and said to Him, "Rabbi, You are the Son of God! You are the King of Israel!" [50] Jesus answered and said to him, "Because I said to you, 'I saw you under the fig tree,' do you believe? You will see greater things than these." [51] And He said to him, "Most assuredly, I say to you, hereafter you shall see heaven open, and the angels of God ascending and descending upon the Son of Man,"" Jesus knew Nathaniel before Philip ever called him; John 4:15-18," The woman said to Him, "Sir, give me this water, that I may not thirst, nor come here to draw." [16] Jesus said to her, "Go, call your husband, and come here." [17] The woman answered and said, "I have no husband." Jesus said to her, "You have well said, 'I have no husband,' [18] for you have had five husbands, and the one whom you now have is not your husband; in that you spoke truly,"" Jesus knew a Samaritan woman married 5 times and lived with a man without marriage, " and in the life of Peter – Acts 5:3, Peter knew Ananian and Sapphira had lied to the Holy Spirit; and in Acts 8:18-23, "And when Simon saw that through the laying on of the apostles' hands the Holy Spirit was given, he offered them money, [19] saying, "Give me this power also, that anyone on whom I lay hands may receive the Holy Spirit." [20] But Peter said to him, "Your money perish with you, because you thought that the gift of God could be purchased with money! [21] You have neither part nor portion in this matter, for your heart is not right in the sight of God. [22] Repent therefore of this your wickedness, and pray God if perhaps the thought of your heart may be forgiven you. [23] For I see that you are poisoned by bitterness and bound by iniquity,"" Peter read what was in Simon's heart through the word of knowledge, and in Paul's life – Acts 27, in verses 21-25, "But after long abstinence from food, then Paul stood in the midst of them and said, "Men, you should have listened to me, and not have sailed from Crete and incurred this disaster and loss. [22] And now I urge you to take heart, for there will be no loss of life among you, but only of the ship. [23] For there stood by me this night an angel of the God to whom I belong and whom I serve, [24] saying, 'Do not be afraid, Paul; you must be brought before Caesar; and indeed God has granted you all those who sail with you.' [25] Therefore take heart, men, for I believe God that it will be just as it was told me," Paul had exercised the word of knowledge to encourage the whole crew, not to be loss of life, who sailed against Paul's warning. The gift is important for the church because it cleanses Church, e.g., Kay's pointing out a fellow's affairs with his secretary. The gift of knowledge can be exercised through the teaching of God word with even a hypothetical case or an example, so that he can give a chance to a convicted person to repent and to convert to God. The Spirit operates in a very natural way.

10. <u>How to Plant a Mulberry Tree in the Ocean</u>

In Hebrews 11:1, the faith is the substance of things hoped for and the evidence of things not seen. The differences between three kinds of faith are described in the Bible: (1) Saving faith is trusting in Jesus Christ as our Savior, believing that He paid the price for our sins; (2) Faith that trusts in the promises of God is the kind of faith growing as we experience the faithfulness of God (Growing Faith); and (3) Healing faith is has a close relationship with the gift of faith, e.g., hemorrhaging woman (Matthew 9:20-22, "And suddenly, a woman who had a flow of blood for twelve years came from behind and touched the hem of His garment. [21] For she said to herself, "If only I may touch His garment, I shall be made well." [22] But Jesus turned around, and when He saw her He said, "Be of good cheer, daughter; your faith has made you well." And the woman was made well from that hour"). Faith is a gift of the Spirit endowing us with the confidence that God is going to work in a specific instance. It is important for the church to walk in faith because the world may see a fresh demonstration of the power of God and thereby be convinced of the reality of Jesus Christ, our risen Lord.

11. Hope for the Sick

All healing comes from God. We are to take concerning healing for the sick by anointing him, laying hands on him, and asking God to heal him. Only explanation for lack of healing is their unbelief and skepticism lead to the lack of healing. In 1 Peter 4:19, "Therefore let those who suffer according to the will of God commit their souls *to Him* in doing good, as to a faithful Creator," we should respond to suffering just by committing to God, because He is doing what He knows to be best.

12. The Hardest Gift to Possess

A miracle is something that He does things we can't explain. Some of miracles recorded in the Old Testament – God parted the Red Sea (Exodus 14, in verse 21,"Then Moses stretched out his hand over the sea; and the LORD caused the sea to go *back* by a strong east wind all that night, and made the sea into dry *land,* and the waters were divided."); Elisha replenished oil to a widow (2 Kings 4 in verse 6,"Now it came to pass, when the vessels were full, that she said to her son, "Bring me another vessel." And he said to her, "*There is* not another vessel." So the oil ceased."); God stopped the Sun in its tracts, so that it did not go down for almost day (Joshua 10 in verse 13, "So the sun stood still, And the moon stopped, Till the people had revenge Upon their enemies. *Is* this not written in the Book of Jasher? So the sun stood still in the midst of heaven, and did not hasten to go *down* for about a whole day. "). And in New Testament – Jesus healed the Centurion's servant from a distance (Matthew 8 in verse 13, "Then Jesus said to the centurion, "Go your way; and as you have believed, *so* let it be done for you." And his servant was healed that same hour."); leper and paralytic healed (Luke 5 in verse 13, "Then He put out *His* hand and touched him, saying, "I am willing; be cleansed." Immediately the leprosy left him," and in verse 25, "Immediately he rose up before them, took up what he had been lying on, and departed to his own house, glorifying God."); and signs and wonder though Stephen's death (Acts 8 in verse 7, "For unclean spirits, crying with a loud voice, came out of many who were possessed; and many who were paralyzed and lame were healed.").   Today, the days of miracles are not over because God is still alive and so still working. Then there will be supernatural happenings. The potential dangers of having the gift of miracles are: (1) to use the gift for personal benefit; and (2) to take his own glory rather than God's glory.   We should earnestly covet the gift of the working of miracles for ourselves and for the church, because it attracted people to the Gospel and offered proof of the Gospel's truth – especially in the area of evangelism.

13. Speaking Forth the Word of God

The gift of prophecy is to speak forth the Word of God through the anointing of the Holy Spirit. This gift is to edify us, to exhort us, and to comfort us in 1 Corinthians 14:3, "But he who prophesies speaks edification and exhortation and comfort to men." Paul gave to Timothy the exhortation concerning this gift, "Do not neglect prophecy."   The office of a prophet is pastors, evangelists, and apostles, while the gift of prophecy can be given to many people within church at God's sovereignty. Paul told to the church concerning the exercise of the gift – conduct decently and in order; let two or three prophets speak and let the others judge. The three scriptural bases for the judging prophecy are: (1) Does the prophecy live with the already revealed Word of God (conflict)?; (2) Does it line up with the fact?; and (3) Does it honor Jesus Christ. We should have a clear understanding of 1 Corinthians 14:32, "...the spirits of the prophets are subject to the prophets," because prophecy is indeed a real blessing to the church for edification, exhortation, comfort and learning.

14. Unmasking the Evil One

It is theoretically possible for two worlds to co-exist at the same time, because the spiritual world is very real, and has a tremendous influence on all of our lives, either for good or for evil. In Ephesians 6:12, "For we do not wrestle against flesh and blood, but against principalities, against powers, against the rulers of the darkness of this age, against spiritual *hosts* of wickedness in the heavenly *place*," the spirit beings are listed as (1) principalities, (2) powers, (3) rulers of the darkness of this age, and (4) spiritual hosts of wickedness in the heavenly places. We need the gift of discerning of spirits, so that we might know whether a man is speaking to us for God, out of his own flesh, or for Satan. The Holy Spirit is able and eager to help us to discern: (1) good from the bad; (2) right from the wrong; and (3) truth from the lies.

15. An Affront to the Intellect; a Blessing to the Soul

The ability given to us through the gift of tongues is to speak fluently in an unknown language through the agency of the Holy Spirit. The gift of tongues expresses the overflowing worship of our spirit and the praise from our heart that we feel toward God. The gift of tongues in the life of the believer assists our prayer life, our devotional life, and edifies himself (not church). But Paul restricted the use of tongues in the church service when an interpreter was present; limited the number of person speaking in tongues during the service; and warned to do tongues decently and in order. Because tongues are not the real issue, the real is how much love and the real manifestation of the Holy Spirit in the life of the believer is by the presence of the Holy Spirit.

16. What Did He Say?

The gift of interpretation of tongues is necessary, because without the gift of interpretation of tongues, an utterance of tongues has no place and no value in a public church service. The difference between interpretation and translation is described as interpretation means explanation of concepts, while translation is word for word transferred. Also, the difference between the gift of interpretation of tongues and the gift of prophecy is described as that is speaking from men to God, while this is form God unto men to edify, exhort, and comfort.

17. Helps – the Quiet Ministry

The gift of helps is so important to the body of Christ, because there are so many things that need to be done if a church is to sustain a full ministry. According to Colossians 3:17, "And *whatever* you do in word or deed, *do* all in the name of the Lord Jesus, giving thanks to God the Father through Him," we are to serve cheerfully whatever we do for the Lord. In the Old Testament, Joshua exercised the gift of helps to Moses, while in the New Testament Timothy exercised the gift of helps to Paul. "Minister" never means "profession, spiritual dictator, or coercive leader" but means "servant (Diakonos, the Greek word: calling of God)," "servant (Leitourgos, the Greek word: unpaid public administrator or volunteer)," and "under rower (Hyperetes, the Greek word). True service is to serve people even in the lowest of tasks as Jesus set the example to seek the will of the Father who sent Jesus. We can find true satisfaction and fulfillment in ministry, not out of the energy of the flesh, but upon the Holy Spirit. God will give us the grace and the strength and the power to serve joyfully. Then, we can find true satisfaction and fulfillment in His ministry.

18. Enough Milk, Already?

According to Ephesians 4:11, "And He Himself gave some *to be* apostles, some prophets, some evangelists, and some pastors and teachers," apostles, prophets, evangelists, pastors, and teachers have been given to the church to instruct in the Word of God. Teaching is a gift of God, and we must depend upon God for its exercise. Paul had the tree-fold ministry – preacher, apostle, and teacher. The difference between the gift of preaching and the gift of teaching is explained as that is for sinners (non-believers) proclaiming Gospel (Good News) and this is for the saints (believers) to grow in the grace and the knowledge of God. Today, the gift of teaching is necessary in the church because more believers will grow and become mature in their relationship with Jesus Christ. The purpose of the gift of teaching is to grow in our relationship and walk with the Lord and for a believer's growth and development. The purpose of the "pastor-teacher" is to equip the saints to minister and to edify the body of Christ till we all come to the unity of the faith and the knowledge of the Son of God, to be perfect.

19. Just Do It!

The body of Christ needs those who exercise the gift of exhortation, because exhorter needs urge our members to do what we know what we should in order to edify the body of Christ. We can know the importance of the gift of exhortation in their lives - James (prove faith by actions), Peter (feed the flock of God; be examples; submit to each other), Paul (present a living sacrifice; pray without ceasing), and Jude (contend earnestly for the faith). Today, the gift of exhortation can work in the church by letting people put into practice the things they have learned from the Scriptures.

20. Keep It Simple

As gravity is a physical law, the law of giving is a spiritual law. God has given the following promises about the principles of giving – (1) for with the same measure that you use, it will be measured back to you (Luke 6:38, "Give, and it will be given to you: good measure, pressed down, shaken together, and running over will be put into your bosom. For with the same measure that you use, it will be measured back to you.""); (2) He who sows bountifully will also reap bountifully (2 Corinthians 9:6, "But this *I say:* He who sows sparingly will also reap sparingly, and he who sows bountifully will also reap bountifully."); (3) Who has first given to Him and it shall be repaid to him (Romans 11:35, "Or who has first given to Him And it shall be repaid to him?"); and (4) If we give to God what is God's and God requires, then the Lord has promised He will pour out blessings to numerous to contain (Malachi 3:10, "Bring all the tithes into the storehouse, That there may be food in My house, And try Me now in this," Says the LORD of hosts, " If I will not open for you the windows of heaven And pour out for you such blessing That there will not be room enough to receive it."). We can explain a guideline to give in 7 ways – 1. Give with simplicity; 2. Give without calling attention to yourself; 3. Give willingly, from the heart; 4. Give cheerfully; 5. Give honestly; 6. Give freely; and 7. Give because of love. We are to give ourselves, our talents and time, and our thanks and praise. The more we give, the more God gives us.

21. An Awesome Responsibility

The highest form of government is theocracy which is a divine monarchy. The name of Israel means "governed by God." Israel was a theocracy. God ruled the nation. Those who take care of the church are elders and deacons. Elders are responsible to take care of spiritual well-being of the church, ruling in the church (controlling their own houses), and letting the deacons handle the material resources of the church, and exercising over the people in matters of spirit. The gift of government has an awesome responsibility because we as rulers are representing God to the people and so we must not misrepresent Him. The ones who can faithfully and/or govern others are filled with the Spirit, having the gift of government. Those are there to find God's decisions and to implement His desires.

22. A Ready Help in Time of Need

The gift of mercy is a divine quality, springing from the very character and nature of God. The difference between justice and mercy is explained as that is exactly what he deserved and this what we don't deserve. The scriptures tell us about the mercy of God – 1. Mercy and forgiveness belong to God (Daniel 9:9, "To the Lord our God *belong* mercy and forgiveness, though we have rebelled against Him."); 2. Abundant in mercy (Numbers 14:18, "'The LORD is longsuffering and abundant in mercy, forgiving iniquity and transgression; but He by no means clears *the guilty,* visiting the iniquity of the fathers on the children to the third and fourth *generation.*'"); 3. His mercy is everlasting (Psalms 100:5, "For the LORD *is* good; His mercy *is* everlasting, And His truth *endures* to all generations."); and 4. Delights in mercy (Micah 7:18, "Who *is* a God like You, Pardoning iniquity And passing over the transgression of the remnant of His heritage? He does not retain His anger forever, Because He delights *in* mercy."). Mercy is listed as one of gifts of the Holy Spirit, because God must plant His mercy in us, not from us. According to Romans 12:8, "he who exhorts, in exhortation; he who gives, with liberality; he who leads, with diligence; he who shows mercy, with cheerfulness," the gift of mercy should be exercised with cheerfulness. Forgiveness is the parallel trait to the gift of mercy, because true forgiveness is real mercy. Showing mercy is a command, not an option, because Jesus commanded us in Luke 6:36, "Therefore be merciful, just as your Father also is merciful."

Part Four – How Should We Respond to the Spirit?

23. The Real Baptism of Fire

The difference between regeneration experience and baptism with the Holy Spirit is described as that experience is conversion, that is, indwelling the Holy Spirit, and this occurs separately subsequently overflowing the Holy Spirit. The Holy Spirit is first "with (para)" us. He begins to dwell "in (en)" us, but as the Lord continues to pour out His Spirit "upon (epi)" us, He begins to overflow from us, this baptism with the Holy Spirit. In Acts 1:8, "But you shall receive power when the Holy Spirit has come upon you; and you shall be witnesses to Me in Jerusalem, and in all Judea and Samaria, and to the end of the earth,"" the purpose of the baptism of the Holy Spirit is witness for Jesus Christ. In the book of Acts, the events occurred in – 1. Baptism with the Spirit followed by tongues (Acts 2 and in verse 4, "And they were all filled with the Holy Spirit and began to speak with other tongues, as the Spirit gave them utterance."); 2. Not yet received the gift of the Holy Spirit (Acts 8 and in verse 16, "For as yet He had fallen upon none of them. They had only been baptized in the name of the Lord Jesus."); 3. Paul's filling with the Holy Spirit distinct from conversion (Acts 9 and in verses 4-5, "Then he fell to the ground, and heard a voice saying to him, "Saul, Saul, why are you persecuting Me?" [5] And he said, "Who are You, Lord?" Then the Lord said, "I am Jesus, whom you are persecuting. It *is* hard for you to kick against the goads.""); 4. The Holy Spirit fell upon all hearing the Word of God taught by Peter (Acts 10 and in verses 43-45, "To Him all the prophets witness that, through His name, whoever believes in Him will receive remission of sins." [44] While Peter was still speaking these words, the Holy Spirit fell upon all those who heard the word. [45] And those of the circumcision who believed were astonished, as many as came with Peter, because the gift of the Holy Spirit had been poured out on the Gentiles also."); and 5. The baptism was an experience subsequent to conversion (Acts 19 and in verse 6, "And when Paul had laid hands on them ["certain disciples" in verse 1], the Holy Spirit came upon them, and they spoke with tongues and prophesied.").

24. <u>Ask and You Shall Receive</u>

The Holy Spirit comes into our lives to help us become holy. We receive the gift of the Holy Spirit by allowing God to fill us His holy presence. Faith is a necessity for receiving the promise of the gift of the Holy Spirit because this gift must be received by faith, not by our work. The Holy Spirit is God's gift to us to enable us to overcome sin, be conformed to the image of Jesus Christ, transform us into a powerful witness for the Lord, and have the power to live for Jesus. We can be confident that we are in God's will when we ask for the fit of the Holy Spirit, by faith of God's promise, "Blessed are those who hunger and thirst for righteousness, for they shall be filled (Matthew 5:6)." We can show God our gratitude for filling us with His spirit, by giving thanks God for His magnificent – e.g., Let Him take our hands and use them to touch the needy, the afflicted, the sick, the suffering; Let Him use our voice to share His love and His truth; Let Him use our heart to love the world around us.

25. A Torrent of Love

Jesus' proclamation in John 7:37-39, "On the last day, that great *day* of the feast, Jesus stood and cried out, saying, "If anyone thirsts, let him come to Me and drink. [38] He who believes in Me, as the Scripture has said, out of his heart will flow rivers of living water." [39] But this He spoke concerning the Spirit, whom those believing in Him would receive; for the Holy Spirit was not yet *given,* because Jesus was not yet glorified," can be explained briefly as "heartily and thirsty believers will flow rivers of living water." Jesus was speaking about human thirst in our spirit for God. It is crucial for our service to God that the Spirit be released as a mighty, gushing torrent, because His objective is always that we be the instruments through which the Holy Spirit might flow forth to the needy world around us. God's Spirit desires to use us by bringing the love of God to others. We can manifest the world which is upside down with God's divine love, in our lives as the Holy Spirit flows forth. The word of "Agape" defines as it is the kind of love that flows forth from our life when we are filled with the Spirit. According to 1 Corinthians 13, the attributes of Agape are stated as in verses 4-8, "Love [Agape] suffers long *and* is kind; love does not envy; love does not parade itself, is not puffed up; [5] does not behave rudely, does not seek its own, is not provoked, thinks no evil; [6] does not rejoice in iniquity, but rejoices in the truth; [7] bears all things, believes all things, hopes all things, endures all things. [8] Love never fails. But whether *there are* prophecies, they will fail; whether *there are* tongues, they will cease; whether *there is* knowledge, it will vanish away." In Galatians 5:22-23, "But the fruit of the Spirit is love, joy, peace, longsuffering, kindness, goodness, faithfulness, [23] gentleness, self-control. Against such there is no law," the fruit (Karphos, the singular form of the Greek Word) of the Spirit is Agape. The terms are used for the fruit as joy, peace, long suffering, kindness, goodness, faithfulness, gentleness, and self-control (8 terms). The genuine evidence of the Holy Spirit within our lives is Agape love.

Epilogue: The Ultimate Experience

The Christian life is the "ultimate experience," because it is hard to describe to a person with no spiritual understanding according to 1 Corinthians 2:14, "But the natural man does not receive the things of the Spirit of God, for they are foolishness to him; nor can he know *them,* because they are spiritually discerned." There is difficulty in explaining spiritual things to the natural man because spiritual things are foolishness to the natural man and he did not know the spiritual things, i.e., he lacks the faculties by which to understand and appreciate the things of Spirit. According to John 15:1-2, ""I am the true vine, and My Father is the vinedresser. ² Every branch in Me that does not bear fruit He takes away; and every *branch* that bears fruit He prunes, that it may bear more fruit," God is looking for the fruit that sprouts from our lives because of our vital relationship with Him. Fruit is produced in the life of a believer, by attaching to the true vine, i.e., not by being cut off from the life of the Spirit. God is looking for the fruit of LOVE in our lives. The source of all our spiritual nourishment and energy is the Spirit. We can contact with God through prayer. God has provided everything we need for life and godliness. Then we just enter and enjoy it. "And do not be drunk with wine, in which is dissipation; but be filled with the Spirit (Ephesians 5:18)"

My thought

Before I got taught the Bible by Chuck, I was afraid of the gift of tongue because I got taught the forbidden gift as stated above in the preface. To edify the body of Christ, God says through Paul in (1) 1 Corinthian 12:10. "to another the working of miracles, to another prophecy, to another discerning of spirits, to another *different* kinds of tongues, to another the interpretation of tongues;" (2) 1 Corinthians 14:2, "For he who speaks in a tongue does not speak to men but to God, for no one understands *him;* however, in the spirit he speaks mysteries;" (3) 1 Corinthians 14:27-28, "[27] If anyone speaks in a tongue, *let there be* two or at the most three, *each* in turn, and let one interpret. [28] But if there is no interpreter, let him keep silent in church, and let him speak to himself and to God;" and (4) 1 Corinthians 14:40, "Let all things be done decently and in order." Thus, I could discern that the gift of tongue is neither prohibited nor allowed without interpreters in a prayer group (at the retreat stated in the preface). Then I prayed to be ready to accept the gift of tongue, which was amazingly given. I am sometimes moved and blessed to pray with tongue in person by the Lord.

Before going to Calvary Chapel, I grew up in the Presbyterian Church (in the preface) where the Board members were elders, elected by the church members, and one senior pastor. But I learned Theocratic church, the church governed by God, in Exodus 18:18-21, "Both you and these people who *are* with you will surely wear yourselves out. For this thing *is* too much for you; you are not able to perform it by yourself. [19] Listen now to my voice; I will give you counsel, and God will be with you: Stand before God for the people, so that you may bring the difficulties to God. [20]

And you shall teach them the statutes and the laws, and show them the way in which they must walk and the work they must do. [21] Moreover you shall select from all the people able men, such as fear God, men of truth, hating covetousness; and place *such* over them *to be* rulers of thousands, rulers of hundreds, rulers of fifties, and rulers of tens." The elders including pastors shall be taught the statues and the laws, which are the Word of God, and must be shown the way in which they must walk. The able men, such as fear God, men of truth, are delegated in deacons who handle material matters. The board members are the elders, who are equipped with the whole counsel of God and are the men of prayers. Only those elders can be qualified candidates to be elected by church members, unlike my previous experience of the Presbyterian Church. Every week at the board prayer meeting, we always pray first on a church matter to seek His will and bring up a relevant Word of God, waiting patiently and flexibly on the Lord in His time. Mostly unanimous decision has been made so far even if it takes a little long because we are hearing of the one and same Spirit's saying to church in Revelation 3:13,"He who has an ear, let him hear what the Spirit says to the churches." Then we pray in conclusion. That's a theocratic government. In Calvary Chapel Pastor Conferences, I met many former Baptists pastors, who affiliated in Calvary Chapel Outreaching Fellowships (CCOF), and talked about their former congregational government of Baptist churches and Moses' seat. Unless all or majority Congressional members are equipped with the whole counsel of God in the direction of the Holy Spirit, their majority decision would be carnal. They could hire or fire a senior pastor at their will rather than at the Bible in the Spirit. So in any other forms of Presbyterian or Episcopal government, the real issue is whether or not decision makers are equipped with the Whole Counsel of God in the work of the Holy Spirit, i.e., whether the church is governed by God.

In "Moses' seat" in Matthew 23:2, "saying: "The scribes and the Pharisees sit in Moses' seat," - like a coercive leader not to do the Word of God which he says - is explained by Jesus in the next verse 3, "Therefore whatever they tell you to observe, *that* observe and do, but do not do according to their works; for they say, and do not do," unlike Calvary Chapel pastors, serving leaders (with servitude heart or Jesus' heart in Philippians 2:5-8, "Let this mind be in you which was also in Christ Jesus, [6] who, being in the form of God, did not consider it robbery to be equal with God, [7] but made Himself of no reputation, taking the form of a bondservant, *and* coming in the likeness of men. [8] And being found in appearance as a man, He humbled Himself and became obedient to *the point of* death, even the death of the cross."). In women's Bible study (called as "a joyful life"), the wife of senior pastor taught the Bible to women at her home. A woman brought a baby, who was crying. The senior pastor took care of the baby while the women were studying, showing the serving pastor. What is a pastor? God says "to edify or build up the Body of Christ" in Ephesians 4:11-12, "And He Himself gave some *to be* apostles, some prophets, some evangelists, and some pastors and teachers, [12] for the equipping of the saints for the work of ministry, for the edifying of the body of Christ" (the bylaws of Calvary Chapel Anaheim Hills attached as a reference in Appendix 2).

1.Self Questions to Confront:

(1) Is every human thought more important than the knowledge of God?

(2) Who is conforming me into the image of Jesus Christ?

(3) Under whose direction, can I preach Christ?

(4) What's the purpose of my prayer?

(5) What does the word of "difference of ministries" mean?

(6) Why is my knowledge without wisdom dangerous?

(7) How does the lack of the gift of wisdom often lead in the Church?

(8) What are three kinds of faith?

(9) What are potential dangers of having the gift of miracles?

(10) How can I judge the prophecy in the Spirit?

(11) What is the gift of tongue?

(12) What do "interpretation" and "minister" mean?

(13) What is the purpose of the "pastor-teacher?"

(14) What is the baptism with the Holy Spirit?

(15) As gravity is a physical law, what is a spiritual law?

(16) What's difference between justice and mercy?

(17) Do I have the genuine evidence of the Holy Spirit in my life?

(18) What's difference between regeneration experience and baptism with the Holy Spirit?

(19) What does the Spirit lead me to do?

(20) What is the real issue of church governments?

2.Verses to Meditate:

(1) 1 John 2:27, "But the anointing which you have received from Him abides in you, and you do not need that anyone teach you; but as the same anointing teaches you concerning all things, and is true, and is not a lie, and just as it has taught you, you will abide in Him."

(2) 1 Corinthians 12:5 "There are differences of ministries, but the same Lord"

(3) Hebrews 11:1 "Now faith is the substance of things hoped for, the evidence of things not seen."

(4) Acts 1:8 "But you shall receive power when the Holy Spirit has come upon you; and you shall be witnesses to Me in Jerusalem, and in all Judea and Samaria, and to the end of the earth."

(5) Galatians 5:22-23 "But the fruit of the Spirit is love, joy, peace, longsuffering, kindness, goodness, faithfulness, [23] gentleness, self-control. Against such there is no law.

(2) Why Grace Changes Everything by Chuck Smith[iv]

The book of "Why Grace Changes Everything" written by Chuck Smith is about we should understand what grace really means. Without grace, our lives are dry and dusty (I experienced as discussed above in the preface). But when grace comes, it transforms our lives into something rich and beautiful. We can never grow in grace by our own efforts, but grace flows from the heart of the Father through the love of Christ. Grace makes life worth living. The book contains the following introduction and fourteen (14) chapters:

A Love Relationship with God

As God has called us into a loving relationship with Himself, our part is to simply trust and believe in the deep care and compassion God freely extends to us. The greatest commandment Jesus says is "Love the Lord with all our heart, mind, soul, and strength, and love our neighbor as ourselves." Love, not the law, is the key to our relationship with God and with one another. The law was intended to serve as a protective guide to God's people, like a parent's safety guidelines, intended only for the welfare of a child. The more we experience God's love, the more He Himself becomes the primary desire and focus of our life. The basis of God's love is Grace, not basis of our works. That Grace makes life worth living. So Grace changes everything in our life.

1. Forgiven!

According to 1 John 1 and in verse 8, "If we say that we have no sin, we deceive ourselves, and the truth is not in us," and in verse 10, "If we say that we have not sinned, we make Him a liar, and His word is not in us," we can deceive ourselves, by blaming others like Adam blaming to Eve, we deceive ourselves because we have no sins. In Romans 3 and in verse 19, "Now we know that whatever the law says, it says to those who are under the law, that every mouth may be stopped, and all the world may become guilty before God," and in verse 23, "for all have sinned and fall short of the glory of God," we have the problem – all have sinned and come short of the glory of God. So, whenever we try to establish our righteousness, by keeping rules, we are forced to admit we operate on a sliding scale. God viewed us in Isaiah 64:6a, "...we are all as an unclean thing, and all our righteousness are as filthy rags." God's requirement for eternal life is our relationship with God totally depends upon God for eternal life, not upon our own being righteous or good. If we are ever to enjoy fellowship with God, "grace" must be applied. According to the New Testament, the word "grace" means God's unmerited favor. Our basis for receiving God's grace and forgiveness into our lives is my belief and trust in God. The gospel of grace is the best news we will ever hear because He loves me and accepts me as I am because I am in Jesus Christ.

2. The Door is Never Closed.

God accounts us to be righteous because we believe in Jesus Christ. The two aspects of the gospel of grace are (1) all of our sins have been taken care of, washed, and forgiven because of our faith in Jesus Christ, and (2) God looks at us as righteous because of our believing in Jesus Christ. But Satan challenges the good news of God's grace if he can cause me to look into myself and at myself. Then, we should respond to the accusation of Satan, "Satan! What you say is true. I know that I have failed. But you don't drive me from Jesus Christ; you are driving me to Him, because my only hope is the Cross of Jesus Christ." It is folly to try to improve on the righteousness that God has imputed to those who believe, because we have believed in Jesus Christ, by not effort, God has imputed the righteousness of Christ to us. "Siamese twins" of the New Testament are "grace and peace" in that order. They are always coupled together because we cannot know the peace of God in our own hearts until we have first experienced the grace of God in our lives. Because Jesus Christ is perfect, I have His righteousness credited to my account because of my faith in Him.

3. No Favorites in the Kingdom

God chooses by His grace whomever He pleases. God prepares each of us for ministry in unique way to each of us. God begins shaping the events and circumstances of our lives for His glory. Preparation is so important to our fulfillment of the special work God has for each of us, because it is necessary that each of us be prepared for that work. But Satan tries to discourage us by using our weakness. Then, we can overcome his condemnation, when we only acknowledge and recognize our weakness and ask God to do for us. We can let Jesus shine forth through our life, our attitudes, our reactions, and our responses.

4. <u>A Portrait of Grace</u>

In Genesis 15 and in verses 4-5, "Then He brought him outside and said, "Look now toward heaven, and count the stars if you are able to number them." And He said to him, "So shall your descendants be." [6] And he believed in the LORD, and He accounted it to him for righteousness," Abraham believed in the Lord and he counted it to him for righteousness. The freedom, the promise, and the blessings of God belong to all those who seek right standing with God through faith in Jesus Christ. God imputes righteousness to our account, when we believe and trust in God. True faith has the result to demonstrate itself in actions. His life is a "glorious picture" of what grace is and does, because it is a stunning portrait of God's love for a sinner who places his complete trust in Him.

5. <u>One Step at a Time</u>

We enjoy deep fellowship with God, by allowing God's Spirit to exercise control over our lives. Walk in the Spirit means we allows the Holy Spirit to exercise control over our lives. We can strengthen the Spirit and walk in the Spirit, while we get more an more into the Word of God by sowing to my spirit and feeding the spirit. The necessity for feeding on God's Word and communing with God through prayer is to become more and more aware of God's presence at all times through His Word, because we deliberately make God our constant companion. The hindrances we face to real spiritual growth in our lives are the flesh, this fallen world system, and Satan himself. Then, we can solve the hindrances, by striving to enter in Christ Jesus at the narrow gate (Philippians 3:14, "I press toward the goal for the prize of the upward call of God in Christ Jesus," and Luke 13:24, "Strive to enter through the narrow gate, for many, I say to you, will seek to enter and will not be able."). We can expect, as we walk in the Spirit, the benefits – our joy in the Lord, peace, a depth of understanding, patience, a kindness, a gentleness, and tremendous victory over even our most besetting sins.

6.   A Garden, Not a Factory

The natural result that we can expect from relationship with Christ is fruits. By their fruits, we can know sheep from wolves. God is interested in what we are, rather than in what we do. Doing is a work of flesh (factory's works). Being is only His work of the Spirit (garden's fruits). Being or bearing fruits is the result of our relationship with God. "The works of God are not wrought because of our righteousness. They are wrought by grace through faith."

7.   Believing for the Blessings

We receive the blessings of God by simply trusting in Him for His blessings because His nature is that He wants to bless us despite unworthy and undeserving us. Many Christians have problems in their Christian experience because God's blessing, they believe, comes from their own righteousness rather than their believing God to bless us. The three promises of blessings to Abraham are - (1) "After these things the word of the LORD came to Abram in a vision, saying, "Do not be afraid, Abram. I *am* your shield, your exceedingly great reward."(Genesis 15:1); (2) "I will make you exceedingly fruitful; and I will make nations of you, and kings shall come from you."(Genesis 17:6); (3) "And I will establish My covenant between Me and you and your descendants after you in their generations, for an everlasting covenant, to be God to you and your descendants after you." (Genesis 17:7). These promises are important to believers because God sees those in Christ and then righteousness of Jesus is imputed to those. The said all blessings are ours when we simply believe God to keep His Word.

8. The Struggle Begins

Our flesh is a terribly strong enemy. In Christian growth, one of the greatest barriers is the notion that we can live a life that pleases God by own efforts, but we can find hope only when we admit our utter powerlessness. The biblical prescription given for resolving the conflict between the flesh and the spirit is not personal discipline or self-control, but the power of the Holy Spirit (Romans 6:6, "knowing this, that our old man was crucified with *Him,* that the body of sin might be done away with, that we should no longer be slaves of sin."). We must do with our specific areas of weakness, by letting the Spirit alone intervene them.

9. Free Indeed!

According to Ephesians 2:3, "among whom also we all once conducted ourselves in the lusts of our flesh, fulfilling the desires of the flesh and of the mind, and were by nature children of wrath, just as the others," we all were incapable of living righteously, because we had no capacity to turn from sin, "all of us were children of wrath…desires of the flesh and mind." We are to use our Christian freedom to serve one another in love. Jesus fulfilled the "golden rule" given in Luke 6:31, "And just as you want men to do to you, you also do to them likewise." In 1 Corinthians 6:12, "All things are lawful for me, but all things are not helpful. All things are lawful for me, but I will not be brought under the power of any," we can maintain our freedom in Christ, (1) not to exercise our freedom in pursing anything and (2) to exercise our freedom to love freely, to serve freely, and to seek freely the best interests of one another.

10. Won't They Go Wild?

The important key we do have for our Christian walk is to trust in Jesus. We are now free from the law, our sinful nature, and our guilt, because the demands of the law were fulfilled when we became crucified with Christ. In our moments of weakness, we can experience victory, by prayer for His help and His strength, the Spirit raises up conviction and power and my mind is turned toward the Lord – my flesh is swallowed up in victory which we experience.   We can choose to do what is right and to refrain from evil, upon God's presence within us (1 John 5:3).   Our relationship with God is steady and secure when we rely upon His constant love, because our relationship isn't based upon us or our performances.

11. Booby Traps and Land Minds

Cults pervert the gospel of Christ in what ways they usually heavily emphasize works and a works-related righteousness. If we preach others – our works or our faithfulness – than gospel (faith in Jesus Christ), we will be cursed to the lowest hell in light of Galatians 1:8, "But even if we, or an angel from heaven, preach any other gospel to you than what we have preached to you, let him be accursed." False teachers frequently used zealously affection or incredible shower of love and attention. If we buy into the false teaching, we end up in bondage of the false teaching under the lordship of men. The best safeguard against this kind of deception is to prove all things; hold fast on which is good, searching the Scriptures.

12. All or Nothing

It is crucial that we stand fast on the truth of God's word because this is the only way to maintain the glorious liberty provided to us so abundantly in Christ. Only a solid grasp of the Scriptures brings real stability to our lives. Paul's exhortation is to stand fast in the liberty wherewith Christ has made us free (Galatians 5:1, "Stand fast therefore in the liberty by which Christ has made us free, and do not be entangled again with a yoke of bondage."). Our righteousness is a result of simple trust in Jesus. We are able to stand in grace, when we search the Scriptures, prove all things, and avoid being taken in by the persuasive arguments of men.

13. Members of Royalty

Paul illustrated the life situation of an heir in Galatians 4 and verses 1-2, "Now I say *that* the heir, as long as he is a child, does not differ at all from a slave, though he is master of all, ² but is under guardians and stewards until the time appointed by the father," until a certain age, he could not enjoy his legal right as an heir under a tutor or guardian. But when a child reached the age specified in a will for a majority, there was no longer a need for a guardian or a steward to exercise oversight. If we are living by the law, we can not expect rich, full, free life of the Holy Spirit, but guilt, condemnation, and frustration. When we are born again spiritually, we can enter into a wonderful, intimate relationship with God. God desires each of us who has the relationship to experience with Him as our Father and who enjoys a close, beautiful, intimate fellowship with God. We can become heirs of God, by coming into this relationship with God as His adopted sons. Because we have been made joint heirs with Jesus, some glorious elements of our inheritance that are ours – full, complete, intimate fellowship with God, son-ship, incorruptible inheritance, spiritual wealth, and member of royalty.

14. Our Sole Responsibility

We are saved by God's grace through faith alone. Righteousness must either come by faith in Christ alone, or by a perfect keeping of God's law. If we seek to be righteous before God by our works, rather than by faith, we find ourselves under a curse. Justification by good works is impossible because it relies on imperfect human effort. If we just believe in Him, He gives us His perfect righteousness. We should not do anything for God, but God has already done for us. So, our sole simple responsibility is to believe in His promise. When we simply place our faith and trust in the work He has done for us, Jesus imparts to us His righteousness. We are saved by grace through faith.

<u>My Thought</u>

In "a Garden, no a Factory," before got taught, I had pursued by own effort to get the best knowledge of environmental protection to please God, feeling emptiness (above in the preface). I was utterly powerless. I did little experience Christian freedom. In John 15:5, ""I am the vine, you *are* the branches. He who abides in Me, and I in him, bears much fruit; for without Me you can do nothing," being or bearing fruits comes from the personal relationship between the Lord Jesus Christ (vine) and me (branch). From the relationship, the more we experience His love (the fruit of the Spirit of Christ), the more He Himself becomes the primary desire and focus of our life. The basis of God's love is Grace, not basis of our works. That Grace makes life worth living. So Grace changes everything in our life, as Grace changed me from my burden by my efforts to the Spirit led life to please God. By allowing God's Spirit to exercise control over our lives, we are enjoying our Christian freedom which the truth, the Word of God, produces, to serve one another in love as Jesus says in John 8:32, "And you shall know the truth, and the truth shall make you free."

In Booby Traps and Land Minds, a pastor in a foreign country came to the States for his personal purpose. He and his companion came to a biblical church for Sunday worship service. He was sick, asking intercessional prayer to the biblical pastor, who prayed for the foreign pastor. The biblical pastor prayed, laying hands on the head of the foreign pastor, which was taken a photograph by the companion. They came back to their home country. Several years later a missionary in the country visited the biblical church in the States, reporting that the foreign pastor planted a church in the name of the biblical church, registering in the foreign country's jurisdiction and advertising the sale of translated books on a newspaper with the photograph without permission of the biblical church. And he ordained women and homosexuals as pastors. Those were never practiced in the biblical church. But such churches used the name of the biblical church were locally misunderstood as a cult to pervert the gospel of Christ. How should the biblical church do against him? Let God do it? The best safeguard against this kind of deception is "searching the Scriptures," rather than hearsays or rumors. From this story, I learned not to conclude fast a judgmental word such as a cult or heresy at hearsays or rumors but to discern acceptable or unacceptable things at the Word of God, discerner, in Hebrews 4:12, "For the Word of God *is* living and powerful, and sharper than any two-edged sword, piercing even to the division of soul and spirit, and of joints and marrow, and is a discerner of the thoughts and intents of the heart." And God will judge us with – reward, no reward, or punishment – accordingly, in light of the counsel of Gamaliel in Acts 5:38-39, "And now I say to you, keep away from these men and let them alone; for if this plan or this work is of men, it will come to nothing; [39] but if it is of God, you cannot overthrow it—lest you even be found to fight against God."

1.Self Questions to Confront:

(1) How can I define "grace?"

(2) What do I have the two aspects of the gospel of grace?

(3)How can I explain the Siamese twins of the New Testament?

(4) How can I overcome Satan's condemnation?

(5) How can I strengthen the Spirit and walk in the Spirit?

(6) What are three promises of blessings to Abraham? How can I have those promises?

(7) Can I live a life that pleases God by own efforts? What's result?

(8) Can I be justified by my good works?

(9) How can I exercise my freedom of Christ?

(10) What is the best safeguard against cults?

2.Verses to Meditate:

(1) John 15:5, ""I am the vine, you *are* the branches. He who abides in Me, and I in him, bears much fruit; for without Me you can do nothing,"

(2) Hebrews 4:12, "For the Word of God *is* living and powerful, and sharper than any two-edged sword, piercing even to the division of soul and spirit, and of joints and marrow, and is a discerner of the thoughts and intents of the heart."

(3) *The Tribulation and the Church by Chuck Smith[v]*

"The Tribulation and the Church" was written by Chuck Smith to examine the biblical reasons why we feel the Church will not be here during the Great Tribulation.

There are two tribulations. One is the great tribulation referred to as the indignation and wrath of God toward His enemies by Jesus (Matthew 24:21-22, "For then there will be great tribulation, such as has not been since the beginning of the world until this time, no, nor ever shall be. [22] And unless those days were shortened, no flesh would be saved; but for the elect's sake those days will be shortened.") and Daniel (Daniel 12:1, "At that time Michael shall stand up, The great prince who stands *watch* over the sons of your people; And there shall be a time of trouble, Such as never was since there was a nation, *Even* to that time. And at that time your people shall be delivered, Every one who is found written in the book."). And it is also detailed by John in Revelation. The other is the tribulation experienced by the child of God comes from the Satan-governed world.

The purpose of the great tribulation is to try men who dwell upon the earth (Revelation 3:10, "Because you have kept My command to persevere, I also will keep you from the hour of trial which shall come upon the whole world, to test those who dwell on the earth."), that God might vent His wrath upon the wicked (Revelation 15:7,"Then one of the four living creatures gave to the seven angels seven golden bowls full of the wrath of God who lives forever and ever."), and to destroy those who destroyed the earth (Revelation 11:18," The nations were angry, and

Your wrath has come, And the time of the dead, that they should be judged, And that You should reward Your servants the prophets and the saints, And those who fear Your name, small and great, And should destroy those who destroy the earth.").   In Romans 5:9, "Much more then, having now been justified by His blood, we shall be saved from wrath through Him,"   in 1 Thessalonians 5:9, "For God did not appoint us to wrath, but to obtain salvation through our Lord Jesus Christ," and in Luke 21:36, "Watch therefore, and pray always that you may be counted worthy to escape all these things that will come to pass, and to stand before the Son of Man," church will not experience the Great Tribulation.

In the 70 weeks of Daniel 9:24-26, "Seventy weeks are determined for your people and for your holy city to finish the transgression.... Until Messiah the Prince there shall be seven weeks and sixty-two weeks..... and after the sixty-two weeks Messiah shall be cut off....shall destroy the city and the sanctuary..,"   each seven represents a 7 years.   The 490 years (70 x 7) refers for Israel.   From March 14, 445 BC when King Artaxerxes of Persia gave the commandment to Nehemiah to restore and rebuild Jerusalem,   it would take 483 years (7x7 + 62x7) which were 173,880 days through 360 days per year on the Babylonian Calendar for Messiah to come first on the earth on April 6, 32 AD. The remaining 7 years between the seventy weeks and the sixty nine weeks are the great tribulation.   So, the church age first between the 69 and 70 week of Daniel's prophecy. The rapture (1 Thessalonians 4:16, "For the Lord Himself will descend from heaven with a shout, with the voice of an archangel, and with the trumpet of God. And the dead in Christ will rise first.") will be caught up the church (Luke 21:36) by Jesus Christ. We will be a metamorphosis in glorified body.   After the rapture, God deal with

Israel, His elect.

In the 70th week, i.e., the Great Tribulation, 144,000 Jews will be sealed by God (Revelation 7:3-4, "saying, "Do not harm the earth, the sea, or the trees till we have sealed the servants of our God on their foreheads." [4] And I heard the number of those who were sealed. One hundred *and* forty-four thousand of all the tribes of the children of Israel *were* sealed") In Revelation 19, the Church as group isn't seen on the earth again in the Book of Revelation, until the Church comes back to earth riding on white horses with Jesus Christ. However, in Revelation 13:7 of "It was granted to him [the beast] to make war with the saints and to overcome them...." the saints refer to Israelites, not to Church, because the beast overcomes the saints. In Matthew 16:18, "And I also say to you that you are Peter, and on this rock I will build My church, and the gates of Hades shall not prevail against it." Therefore, the saints must be Israel which are also the "elect" of Matthew 24:31, "And He will send His angels with a great sound of a trumpet, and they will gather together His elect from the four winds, from one end of heaven to the other."

In 2 Thessalonians 2:7, "For the mystery of lawlessness is already at work; only He who now restrains *will do so* until He is taken out of the way, "the force of "restraints" is the power the Holy Spirit working in and through the Church. When the church has been removed and is rejoicing with the Lord in Heaven, restrains are not on the earth and the wicked one takes over the world.

The trump of God or the last trumpet, in 1 Thessalonians 4:16," For the Lord Himself will descend from heaven with a shout, with the voice of an archangel, and with the trumpet of God. And the dead in Christ will rise first," and 1 Corinthians 15:52," in a moment, in the twinkling of an eye, at the last trumpet. For the trumpet will sound, and the dead will be raised incorruptible, and we shall be changed," in light of "glorified body" is different from the 7th trumpet in Revelation 10 in light of "woe, woe, woe" in the Revelation 8:13, "And I looked, and I heard an angel flying through the midst of heaven, saying with a loud voice, "Woe, woe, woe to the inhabitants of the earth, because of the remaining blasts of the trumpet of the three angels who are about to sound!" because no reason exists to define the last trump to be the 7th trumpet as well as to assume no trumpets after the last trump of 1 Corinthians 15.

In Revelation 20:4, "And I saw thrones, and they sat on them, and judgment was committed to them. Then *I saw* the souls of those who had been beheaded for their witness to Jesus and for the Word of God, who had not worshiped the beast or his image, and had not received *his* mark on their foreheads or on their hands. And they lived and reigned with Christ for a thousand years." There are two different companies in the 1st resurrection for the just. One is that thrones seen by John and those who sat upon them are raptured church. The other company is that the souls of those beheaded for the witness of Jesus are resurrected. In the 2nd resurrection, the unjust stands before the Great White Throne judgment of God in Revelation 20:11-14," Then I saw a great white throne and Him who sat on it, from whose face the earth and the heaven fled away. And there was found no place for them. ^{12} And I saw the dead, small and great, standing before God, and books were opened. And another book was opened, which is *the Book* of Life. And the dead were judged according to their works, by the things which were written in the books. [13] The sea gave up the dead who were in it, and Death and Hades delivered up the dead who were in them. And they were judged, each one according to his works. [14] Then Death and Hades were cast into the lake of fire. This is the second death."

In Daniel 12:11, "And from the time *that* the daily *sacrifice* is taken away, and the abomination of desolation is set up, *there shall be* one thousand two hundred and ninety days," Christ will would be returning for the judgment in 1,290 days from abomination of desolation set up at 3 ½ years during the great tribulation. In Daniel 12:12, "Blessed *is* he who waits, and comes to the one thousand three hundred and thirty-five days," Christ will function millennial kingdom 1,335 days from the midpoint of the great tribulation.

But we don't know exact day in Matthew 24:36, "the day and hour no one knows, no, not even the angles of heaven, but My Father only." However, we are ready for the Son of Man coming at an hour when we do not expect Him in Matthew 24:44," Therefore you also be ready, for the Son of Man is coming at an hour you do not expect." Thus, we should be faithful like the church of Philadelphia in Revelation 3:10, "Because you have kept My command to persevere, I also will keep you from the hour of trial which shall come upon the whole world, to test those who dwell on the earth." The only divine preservation is for 144,000 Israelites who are sealed in the Great Tribulation.

The vast majority of biblical Christians throughout the world – for we truly believe that Jesus Christ is coming soon, and we look for Him to take us out of this wicked world system at any time. We should not quit our works because Jesus said, "Occupy till I come" (Luke 19:13, KJV, "And he called his ten servants, and delivered them ten pounds, and said unto them, Occupy till I come.").

My Thought

Before got taught, I never heard of sermons from Chapter 6 through 18 in the book of Revelation. Chuck with this book taught the book of Revelation, which is Jesus' revelation, containing past (Chapter 1), present (Chapter 2 and 3), and future period (Chapter 4 through 22). In the future period, Chapters 4 and 5 talk about the church caught up with the Lord in heaven (raptured church, the 1st part of 1st resurrection of believers). Concurrently on the earth, Chapters 6 through 18 talk about the 7 years Great Tribulation. Thereafter, Chapter 19 ends with Armageddon by Christ's 2nd coming on earth. Chapter 20 talks the 2nd part of the 1st resurrection of beheaded Jews (144,000), Millennium Kingdom, and the 2nd resurrection of unbelievers on the great white throne judgment. Chapter 21 and 22 talk new heaven and new earth for eternal kingdom. The church's rapture will occur literally before the great tribulation, called as pre-tribulation. Also the church's rapture will occur before the Millennium Kingdom, called as "pre-millennium." As Jesus says in Matthew 24:36, "the day and hour no one knows, no, not even the angles of heaven, but My Father only," I don't speculate any exact time for rapture but I am looking for Jesus Christ coming, "at an hour I do not expect," in Matthew 24:44, soon, to take us into heaven out of this wicked world system at any time. Upon this faith of Jesus' coming again soon, my life is changed as follows: (1) I can be raptured during my life

(2) I can have a constant exceeding hope to meet our Lord soon, joyfully. (3) I am constrained with AGAPE to preach to unbelievers more and more before His urgent coming. (4) The priority of my life is always the Kingdom of God or eternal things over temporary or earthly thing. (5) I am purified or sanctified to the image of Christ who is coming soon.

1.Self Questions to Confront:

(1) Do I believe to be caught up with the Lord in heaven?

(2) When is Jesus coming again? Am I ready for His coming?

(3) Is my life changed upon faith of Jesus' 2nd coming soon in Matthew 24:44? How is it changed?

2.Verses to Meditate:

(1) 1 Thessalonians 4:16, "For the Lord Himself will descend from heaven with a shout, with the voice of an archangel, and with the trumpet of God. And the dead in Christ will rise first."

(2) Matthew 24:44," Therefore you also be ready, for the Son of Man is coming at an hour you do not expect."

---

(4) Five Points of Calvinism by George Bryson[vi]

In the book of "Five Points of Calvinism" written by George Bryson, he was treated to be Calvinists by other Calvinists because Calvary Chapel are relying solely on the Bible. Some parts of the Bible are similar to the Calvinism, but the other parts of the Bible are different. Here are the following five (5) points of Calvinism, comparing to the Bible.

Total Depravity

When man is born, he totally is depraved. And man must be born again so you can believe, so that faith is a consequence of regeneration. However, according to John 1:12-13, "But as many as received Him, to them He gave the right to become children of God, to those who believe in His name: [13] who were born, not of blood, nor of the will of the flesh, nor of the will of man, but of God," man must believe so tat he can be born again. Therefore, faith is the precondition of regeneration.

Unconditional Election

Man is elected by God regardless of any condition including even faith in Christ. However, according to John 3:16-17, "For God so loved the world that He gave His only begotten Son, that whoever believes in Him should not perish but have everlasting life. [17] For God did not send His Son into the world to condemn the world, but that the world through Him might be saved," man is elected by God in accordance with faith in Christ.

Limited Atonement

Christ died with blood shed on the cross to put away the sin, limited to the elect, i.e., Christ died only for the elect. However, according to 1 John 2:2, "And He Himself is the propitiation for our sins, and not for ours only but also for the whole world," Christ died for all the lost, not only elect but also non-elect.

Irresistible Grace

God's grace is "unmerited favor." That grace is not able to be resisted by the elect, so that God appears to offer salvation to all the elect. Salvation is insured for the elect regardless of the faith or willingness of the elect. The elect can't help but believe and be eventually saved, and the unelected cannot help but not believe and be ultimately damned. However, in Romans 1:16, "For I am not ashamed of the gospel of Christ, for it is the power of God to salvation for everyone who believes, for the Jew first and also for the Greek," God truly offers salvation to everyone on the condition that he believes in Jesus Christ. The saved can thank God for the provision of salvation (the cross), the offer of salvation which is the gospel proclamation, the nature of the offer, i.e., free gift, and the capacity to believe in Christ and thereby receive the free gift. Those ultimately lost will have only themselves to blame.

Perseverance of the Saints

The saved or saints among the elect will persevere in holiness and faith to the end of their life on earth, thereby proving they are among the elect. Those who do not persevere in faith and holiness until the end have proved they were never saved and thus not among the elect. However, according to John 15:1-14 "(1) I am the true vine, and My Father is the vinedresser ... (7) If you abide in Me, and My words abide in you, you will ask what you desire, and it shall be done for you...... (14)You are My friends if you do whatever I command you," the saved should persevere in faith and holiness to the end of their lives on earth. But although saved, they might experience a loss of fellowship with Jesus Christ on earth and a loss of rewards in the next.

<u>My Thought</u>

After reading, the thought of John Calvin should be subject to understand the knowledge of God to the obedience of our Lord. Since 16th Century, different thoughts between John Calvin (1509-1564) and Jacob Hermann (1560-1609)[vii] have been called as Calvinism and Arminianism respectively, producing denominational churches. Presbyterian and Reformed churches were influenced by Calvinism while Methodist and Pentecostal churches were influenced by Armianism. Unfortunately, historically their over-emphasis of doctrinal differences has led to the division of the body of Christ as I felt the turmoil of denominations in my early Christian life (above). Because our Christians' basis is His love, which is greater than any difference, we should not polarize the difference into division but focus on the Bible talking about the Lord Jesus Christ as Jesus says in John 5:39, "You search the Scriptures, for in them you think you have eternal life; and these are they which testify of Me."

For total depravity, God says through Paul in Romans 3:23, "for all have sinned and fall short of the glory of God." I agreed with John before a man is born again upon his faith in Jesus Christ. On the other hand, God says in Romans 3:26, "to demonstrate at the present time His righteousness, that He might be just and the justifier of the one who has faith in Jesus." A nurse working for a physician at a clinical office treated mistakenly a patient. Then, her mistake or fault is imputed to her physician because of the relationship between an employer and employee. Likewise, a person's relationship with God the Father is restored upon his faith in Jesus. Because of the relationship, Jesus' righteousness is imputed to the person. So, because of the whole work of Jesus the justifier, he is no longer totally depraved but is justified, although he is in a spiritual warfare between his total depravity or carnality to be mortified and spirituality to be confirmed with the image of Jesus in light of Romans 7:24-8:1(KJV),"O wretched man that I am! who shall deliver me from the body of this death? [25]I thank God through Jesus Christ our Lord. So then with the mind I myself serve the law of God; but with the flesh the law of sin. [1]There is therefore now no condemnation to them which are in Christ Jesus, who walk not after the flesh, but after the Spirit." Therefore, faith is the concurrent condition of regeneration because upon faith, not after faith, regeneration starts at the same time as faith.

In Unconditional Election, God says in John 3:16, "For God so loved the world that He gave His only begotten Son, that whoever believes in Him should not perish but have everlasting life." Since everlasting life is much longer than the time to have a person's faith in Jesus during his physical life, faith is a condition for everlasting life. (1) The condition is concurrent because as long as any one believes in Jesus, he has everlasting life. (2) If a person believes in Christ, he shall have everlasting life, or just after his faith condition suffices he shall be elected or saved. That's condition precedent giving a time of his work to his salvation beyond God's sovereignty contrary to Ephesians 2:8, "For by grace you have been saved through faith, and that not of yourselves; *it is* the gift of God". (3) Everyone is elected, unless he rejects Christ, which is condition subsequent. Everyone who is born physically is elected or saved (universal election) but his rejection of Christ causes the loss of election. Here a historical tedious question is raised whether or not salvation may be lost. The salvation's determination is absolutely up to God. Only God knows the salvation, securing believers as known of "the believer's security of salvation" in John 10:28, "And I give them eternal life, and they shall never perish; neither shall anyone snatch them out of My hand," but my answer[viii] is limited to the present question (discussed above in the preface), whether or not a man is saved now, as 2 Corinthians 13:5, "Examine yourselves *as to* whether you are in the faith. Test yourselves. Do you not know yourselves, that Jesus Christ is in you?—unless indeed you are disqualified."

The person can exercise the free will, given by God, to believe in Jesus by hearing of Gospel. The free will is under God's sovereignty as Adam was given the free will to exercise to choose every tree and/or the forbidden tree of knowledge of good and evil in Genesis 2:16-17, "And the LORD God commanded the man, saying, "Of every tree of the garden you may freely eat; but of the tree of the knowledge of good and evil you shall not eat, for in the day that you eat of it you shall surely die." God doesn't accept a forced obedience rather than a willing obedience in 2 Corinthians 8:12, "For if there is first a willing mind, *it is* accepted according to what one has, *and* not according to what he does not have." The "freewill" term is stated 17 times in the KJV Bible (e.g. "freewill offerings"). I taught the Bible to a member whose faith came by hearing and hearing by the Word of God. But after she suffered Alzheimer's disease, her faith little came. A lot of portion of her free will to hear is taken away by sovereign God. Even free will is almost negligible compared to sovereign God who creates earth and universe but is still existent until God takes it away. Therefore, there is no conflict between human free will and God's sovereignty because the free will is given by Sovereign God. So, I have a different thought in part from unconditional election, as man is elected by God in concurrent condition of faith in Christ.

For limited atonement, Christ's death with blood shed for all the lost, not only elect but also non-elect, is given opportunity of atonement for all the lost, but man can exercise the given free will to either accept or reject Christ, which is, to either believe in Christ or not. A widow made a will to devise her 100 acres farm land in Texas to her sole son who lived in New York. Upon her death, he received the will but rejected to inherit the 100 acres farm, conveying intestate to her next kin who accepted it. Likewise, Christ's atonement is limited to man's acceptance of Christ. Christ's atonement is limited to man's faith in the Lord Jesus Christ. The opportunity of atonement given to all people upon Jesus' death with blood shed is different from both the atonement limited to the elect (Calvinism) and universal atonement (Arminianism) known as redemption of everybody.

For Irresistible Grace, God says in Ephesians 2:8, "For by grace you have been saved through faith, and that not of yourselves; *it is* the gift of God." God's grace is freely given unmerited favor and so God's grace for salvation solely upon faith, not any merits or work in human part. So, I have the same thought as George's thought, different from obstructable Grace (Arminianism) explained as "God's grace for salvation is to all men unless absolute man's free will frustrates it." Here a historical tedious question is again stated above.

For Perseverance of the Saints, no condemnation is to those who are in Jesus Christ but those may be Carnal Christians rather than Spiritual Christians as Paul sent a letter to Corinthians in 1 Corinthians 3:1, "And I, brethren, could not speak to you as to spiritual *people* but as to carnal, as to babes in Christ." So, I have a different thought in part from Calvin, in whole from falling grace (Arminianism) known as "man cannot continue in salvation grace unless he continues to will to be saved," but the same thought as George's, although they are saved ones, they might experience a loss of fellowship with Jesus Christ on earth and a loss of rewards in the next, as Paul says in 1 Corinthians 3:15, "If anyone's work is burned, he will suffer loss; but he himself will be saved, yet so as through fire."

Every thought should be subject to the Bible itself. The Bible itself existence is not subject to Calvinism or Arminianism or any other Protestants' human thoughts which thereafter came out in the 15th century. When some points are not understood, I am waiting on the Lord's revelation. I think that Calvinism is a thought over-emphasizing the God's characteristics of sovereignty, fore-knowledge, and predestination but wiping out human free will, while Arminanism is a thought over-emphasizing human free will wiping out the God's characteristics, although the Bible states both. Each over emphasizing portion is a man-made-frame different from all Scripture given by inspiration of God. I don't polarize but I accept as the Bible is.

1.Self Questions to Confront:
  (1) What does TULIP stand for?
  (2) How can I be saved?

(3) Am I saved?

(4) Is my faith the concurrent condition for election?

2.Verses to Meditate:

(1) 1 John 2:2, "And He Himself is the propitiation for our sins, and not for ours only but also for the whole world."

(2) Ephesians 2:8-9, "For by grace you have been saved through faith, and that not of yourselves; *it is* the gift of God, [9] not of works, lest anyone should boast."

(3) 2 Corinthians 13:5, "Examine yourselves *as to* whether you are in the faith. Test yourselves. Do you not know yourselves, that Jesus Christ is in you?—unless indeed you are disqualified"

(5) The Psychologizing of the Faith by Bob Hoekstra [ix]

"The Psychologizing of the Faith," written by pastor Bob Hoekstra talks about the wonderful counselor, Jesus Christ, in the Word of God, rather than human experts in psychological theory for counseling and direction for the lives of Christians.

<u>The redefining Process</u>

The intrusion of psychological thinking into the church of the Lord Jesus Christ is a compromise between world and church.

The Ministry of Counseling

The counseling needs the direction of God rather than of the world experts, because sheep (Christians) need a shepherd to guide us through life. All of the necessary wisdom and knowledge for life and godliness is all found in Christ. When we allow the Son of God to counsel us through God's word, we develop a personal relationship with Him. We should be careful for so called Christian counselors because they generally have been trained in the same psychological theories as the secular therapists of the world because they typically integrate the human speculations of godless theories of Sigmund Freud, Car Jung, Abraham Maslow, Erich Fromm, and others, who are in contrary to Christ and to His Word. Only God can look on the heart of man, evaluate it, and supply the remedy for the needs of the heart. In order to God mercifully work in us, we must not neglect the commands, provisions, and warnings of God. Jesus Christ as our Wonderful Counselor calls the church to His perfect ways instead of to the ways of man.

The Problem of Sin

We should focus on Jesus Christ via the Word of God because all men have sinned. But upon our faith, the Lord Jesus Christ leads to the gift of eternal life. This is God's grace which is much more than we need. While we walk in the wholeness of Christ instead of in the brokenness of man, we overcome the world, the flesh, and the devil. Only God can deal with the ultimate problem of sin. Sadly, the sin is being psychologically redefined in many churches today.

The Call of Discipleship

We are all called to be disciples of the Lord Jesus. A disciple is a follower, one who follows a master and teacher. Deny self such as self-centeredness, self-righteousness, self-help, self-hope, etc. Take up our cross – make the cross of Christ our cross, cling to it, and hope in it as our only remedy for our sins. Keep a daily way of life, following Jesus. Denying self and esteeming self are two opposite directions. One is humility, and the other is pride. One is God's way and the other is man's way. We need "Christ esteem." Following Jesus, we are to learn increasingly to hold Him in high regard.

The Sufficiency of Christ

Sufficiency comes from Christ. Its foundation is the faith unlike so called psychologizing of the faith enticing people away from the full provision of God. The fruits of the Holy Spirit are love, peace, joy, goodness, kindness, faithfulness, meekness, and self-control. Ministering His life to one another as God's people is all related to the sufficiency of Christ.

The Sufficiency of God's Word

God's word is sufficient because in 2 Timothy 3:16-17 "All scripture is given by inspiration of God, and is profitable for doctrine, for reproof, for correction, for instruction in righteousness, that the man of God may be complete, thoroughly equipped for every good work." The Word of God is inspired and has God's authority. Since the Word makes men complete, thoroughly equipped for every good work, the Word is sufficient to make our lives what God wants our lives to be – saved, sanctified, and fully equipped for service.   All truth is God's truth unlike human theories.

The Work of the Holy Spirit

The Holy Spirit guides us into all the truth of the Word of God.   The Spirit transforms our images to much more like God's images – human characters changed.   All theories out of men is apart from the faith, once for all delivered to the saints.

The Supreme Goal of knowing God.

Knowing God is superior to any human theories. Grace and peace is multiplied to us in the knowledge of God and of Jesus our Lord.   The more we know the Lord, the more we provides for godliness.

The Great Commandment to Love God

First we must love God. Then men must love others, not love ourselves, which is false teaching added to the Word of God.   Thus, self-love is in danger.

Concluding Evaluation

Turning from Jesus Christ who is sufficient for our life, to the broken cisterns of psychological theories is evil.   Simplicity in Christ may be corrupted by the psychological theories because the whole kingdom of

God is simply wrapped up in Jesus Christ but the psychological theories are complicated, deceitful, and futile. Also philosophy is man's way of viewing man and life and how to help and/or change people, no mater how well educated, which is of this world, but God's kingdom is not of this world (John 18:36," Jesus answered, "My kingdom is not of this world. If My kingdom were of this world, My servants would fight, so that I should not be delivered to the Jews; but now My kingdom is not from here."""). Thus, Special measures of human genius, like Freud, Adler, Jung, Maslow, Fromm, Rogers, and on and on, are futile, useless, vain, or empty. Only Jesus and His ways and His truth are to be guiding and shaping our life. We are called to proclaim the Word of God, not man's theories (mythic, humanistic, psychological concepts). Teach the Word of God! Keep the Word in our life, church, and ministry! Let the Holy Spirit work in our life through the Word. Then, He can give us the insight, discernment, wisdom, courage, alertness, and love.

My Thought

I am a born again Christian, who abides in the Word of God, called as His disciple in John 8:31,"Then Jesus said to those Jews who believed Him, "If you abide in My word, you are My disciples indeed."" In John 14:26, "But the Helper, the Holy Spirit, whom the Father will send in My name, He will teach you all things, and bring to your remembrance all things that I said to you," I should abide in His word as the Spirit teaches "ALL" things that Jesus said to me. We as His disciples should not compromise with the World, the psychological theory in the World. This book is like the biblical counseling. Whenever problems are counseled, we should bring the Word of God close to the situation of the person counseled. Let the Holy Spirit work in the counseled person who is a born-again Christian. If not a Christian, let him hear of Gospel. All human theories must be subordinate to the Word of God to be understood faithfully for His thought. If there is any conflict among them, always the Word of God will prevail over anything else because the Word of God is absolute true. If a Christian's brain itself is physically damaged due to a car accident or aging, a psychiatrist prescribing medicine should be taken by him within the scope of God.

1.Self Questions to Confront:

  (1) Am I Jesus' disciple?　Why?

  (2) What types of self should I deny?

  (3) Who guides me into the truth of the Word of God?

2.Verses to Meditate:

  (1) John 8:31, "Then Jesus said to those Jews who believed Him, "If you abide in My word, you are My disciples indeed."

  (2) John 14:26, ""But the Helper, the Holy Spirit, whom the Father will send in My name, He will teach you all things, and bring to your remembrance all things that I said to you,"

(6) *Calvary Chapel Distinctives by Chuck Smith*[x]

The book of "Calvary Chapel Distinctives" written by Chuck Smith who is the senior pastor of Calvary Chapel at Costa Mesa, has ministered from the youth revolution of the '60s and '70s into what has become a nationwide group of Calvary Chapel churches and of radio, *The Word For Today,* shows that the balance between the teaching of the Word of God and an open heart to the work of the Holy Spirit makes Calvary Chapel Movement distinct, unique, and different from the other churches in the following fifteen (15) chapters:

Preface

The Calvary Chapel movement has a strong emphasis on teaching the Word of God as well as an open heart to the work of the Holy Spirit (influence on my life as well as on this book). God created a wide variety of churches in the balance between the Word and the Work of the Holy Spirit.

The Call To The Ministry

Under Hebrews 5:4 "...this honor...he that is called of God...," God has called us - as ministers, not professions, to serve Him. Chuck had financial difficulty and consequently spiritual difficulty for 17 years. He found that the ministry was His ministry, not his own ministry based upon own ambitions, own desires, and own will. Under 1 Peter 2:21, "For to this you were called, because Christ also suffered for us, leaving us an example, that you should follow His steps," Chuck discovered the ministry was service, not being served.   Chuck was serving Him, picking up cigarette butt down anywhere (one time I saw, discussed above in the testimonial preface) under Colossians 3:17 "And *whatever* you do in word or deed, *do* all in the name of the Lord Jesus, giving thanks to God the Father through Him." To present day, he has not looked for the applause of people or people to say but has committed to serve His people, to the Word of God, and to study the Word of God, so as to show himself approved unto God.

God's Model For the Church

Under Matthew 16:18, "And I also say to you that you are Peter, and on this rock I will build My church, and the gates of Hades shall not prevail against it."   Chuck said that church history showed imperfect Christianity examples, so that the model of church should be found in the book of Acts. The church was filled with the Holy Spirit, led by the Holy Spirit and empowered by the Holy Spirit, developing oneness via fellowship and koinonia. In Acts 2:42, "And they continued steadfastly in the apostles' doctrine and fellowship, in the breaking of bread, and in prayers," the early church had 4 basic functions – continuance of the apostles' doctrine, fellowship, breaking of bread and prayers. During this course, in Acts 2:47, "praising God and having favor with all the people. And the Lord added to the church daily those who were being saved," the Lord added to the church daily, such as should be saved.   Likewise, for the growth of church, faithful ministers should get the people into the Word, in prayer, in fellowship, and in the breaking of bread. Then, God will add to the church daily that should be saved, regardless of the human efforts to grow church (stated "McChurch" in the preface above).   Ministers should not seek their own glory but bring glory unto Jesus, living for the kingdom of God. The church in the book of Acts is God's Model for the Church.

Church Government

Under Ephesians 1:22 "And has put all things under His feet, and gave Him to be the head over all things to the church," Calvary Chapel's church government adopts that the head of Church is Jesus Christ. It is called theocracy, which is God-ruled government. The senior pastor is ruled by the Lord and aided by the Elders and the Assistant Pastors to discover the mind and will of Jesus Christ for His Church. This is like the relationship between Moses directed by God and Aaron and priesthood beyond congregation. Calvary Chapel did not adopt overseers government (1 Timothy 3:1, "This *is* a faithful saying: If a man desires the position of a bishop, he desires a good work.") and elders government (Acts 14:23, "So when they had appointed elders in every church, and prayed with fasting, they commended them to the Lord in whom they had believed.") because they could hire or fire pastors who become hirelings. Congregational government has no biblical basis but in Exodus 16:2, "Then the whole congregation of the children of Israel complained against Moses and Aaron in the wilderness," and in Numbers 14:1-3, "So all the congregation lifted up their voices and cried, and the people wept that night. ² And all the children of Israel complained against Moses and Aaron, and the whole congregation said to them, "If only we had died in the land of Egypt! Or if only we had died in this wilderness! ³ Why has the LORD brought us to this land to fall by the sword, that our wives and children should become victims? Would it not be better for us to return to

Egypt?"" they were murmuring congregation against Moses and Aaron in the wilderness.

Empowered by the Spirit

In Acts 1:8, "But you shall receive power, when the Holy Spirit has come upon you; and you shall be witnesses to Me in Jerusalem, and in all Judea, and in Samaria, and to the end of the earth," Calvary Chapel believes 3 kinds of experiences with the Holy Spirit – (1) *in*dwelling of the Holy Spirit at conversion ("en," 1 Corinthians 6:19-20 "Or do you not know that your body is the temple of the Holy Spirit *who is* in you, whom you have from God, and you are not your own? [20] For you were bought at a price; therefore glorify God in your body and in your spirit, which are God's."), beyond the Holy Spirit dwelling **with** you ("para," John 14:16-17 "And I will pray the Father, and He will give you another Helper, that He may abide with you forever— [17] the Spirit of truth, whom the world cannot receive, because it neither sees Him nor knows Him; but you know Him, for He dwells with you and will be in you."), (2) filled up the holy spirit or baptism with the Holy Spirit (Acts 10) (3) Overflowing with the the Holy Spirit, the gift of the Spirit, or empowering of the Spirit, or the Holy Spirit **upon** you ("epi, Acts 1:8").

Building the Church God's Way

In Zechariah 4:6, "…Not by might nor by power, but by My Spirit, Says the Lord of hosts," Calvary Chapel simply trusts in the work of the Holy Spirit, and of Jesus Christ who is building His church as He said He would, because the Word of God from Genesis through Revelation is alive and powerful and ministers to the spirit of the people, although the people of Calvary Chapel wear a relaxed casual style suits and disregard any human fund raiser to build the church.

Grace upon Grace

In Hebrews 13:9, "Do not be carried about with various and strange doctrines. For *it is* good that the heart be established by grace, not with foods which have not profited those who have been occupied with them," Calvary Chapel experiences God's grace daily and each member is saved by it personally. We believe that the Bible does teach that God is gracious beyond legalism such as in 'reformation theology.' We believe that God is sovereign and a man is responsible and that God holds him responsible for the choices that he makes (with his free will), not taking polarizing position such as Calvinism. We simply trust that both assertions of Scripture are true.

The Priority of the Word

In Timothy 4:13, "Till I come, give attendance to reading, to exhortation, to doctrine," and in Acts 20:27, "For I have not shunned to declare to you the whole counsel of God," Calvary Chapel declares the whole counsel of God to people, which means Calvary Chapel teaches its congregation members the whole Word of God as the priority of the Word, based upon verse by verse inductive sermon – not topical sermons.

The Centrality of Jesus Christ

In 2 Corinthians 4:5, "For we do not preach ourselves, but Christ Jesus the Lord, and ourselves your bondservants for Jesus' sake," Calvary Chapel has the centrality of Jesus Christ in its worship, not allowing any distraction to focus on Him such as standing up individually, because stood people really made attention to themselves from the congregation rather than they gave glory for Jesus Christ in 1 Corinthians 1:29 "that no flesh should glory in His presence" like Ananias and Sapphira.

The Rapture of the Church

In Titus 2:13, "Looking for the blessed hope, and the glorious appearing of the great God and Savior Jesus Christ," Calvary Chapel believes that the blessed hope of the glorious appearing of the great God and Savior Jesus is the spark today that God has used to bring revival through the church. In detail, in 1 Thessalonians 4:16-18, "For the Lord Himself shall descend from heaven with a shout, with the voice of the archangel, and with the trump of God: and the dead in Christ shall rise first: Then we which are alive and remain shall be **caught up** together with them in the clouds, to meet the Lord in the air: and so shall we ever be with the Lord," the rapture of church, which is Jesus coming for His church, will occur 1st. Great Tribulation will occur 2nd for 7 years and then the Antichrist established Satan's kingdom in full power in the Parable of the Ten Virgins of Matthew 25 and in verses 1-3, ""Then the kingdom of heaven shall be likened to ten virgins who took their lamps and went out to meet the bridegroom. [2] Now five of them were wise, and five *were* foolish. [3] Those who *were* foolish took their lamps and took no oil with them." Church will not go through the Great Tribulation in Luke 21:36, "Watch therefore, and pray always that you may be counted worthy to escape all these things that will come to pass, and to stand before the Son of Man." Jesus coming with His church on the earth will occur 3rd in Colossians 3:4, "When Christ, who is our life, shall appear (at His 2nd coming), then you also will appear with Him in glory." Be ready! The Lord is coming for His people, and He is going to take us to be with Him.

Having Begun in the Spirit

In 2 Corinthians 3:5-6, "Not that we are sufficient of ourselves to think of anything as *being* from ourselves, but our sufficiency *is* from God, [6] who also made us sufficient as ministers of the new covenant, not of the letter but of the Spirit; for the letter kills, but the Spirit gives life," Calvary Chapel is a work which was begun in the Holy Spirit. Its movement is alive in the Spirit but dead in ritualism as found in Church history. Only when you are to continue in the Spirit, God fills us with His Spirit, and does mighty work through us that astounds and beats the world.

The Supremacy of Love

In John 13:35, "By this all will know that you are My disciples, if you have love for one another," Calvary Chapel believes that God's supreme desire for us is that we experience His love and then share that love with others because without love all the gifts and powers of the Holy Spirit are meaningless and worthless. "Herein is my Father glorified, that you bear much fruit; so shall you be my disciples. As the Father has loved me, so have I loved you: continue you in my love." (John 15:8-9). So we can vividly see the supremacy of love.

Striking the Balance

In 2 Timothy 2:15, "Be diligent to present yourself approved to God, a worker who does not need to be ashamed, rightly dividing the word of truth," Calvary Chapel has desire not to divide God's people over non-essential issues. We are able to minister to as broad a group of people as possible, so that we are neither Pentecostal view nor Baptist view, neither Five Point Calvinists nor Arminians. We do believe (1) that we can't lose our salvation, that we need to persevere because we are saints in John 8:31,"Then Jesus said to those Jews who believed Him, "If you abide in My word, you are My disciples indeed," (2) that Jesus died for everybody, (3) that God has totally sovereignty, and (4) that God has given us the capacity of choice. We do not try to bring God within the confines of our intellect, accepting the limitlessness of God and getting the Word of God in a well-balanced spiritual diet.

Ventures of Faith

In Hebrews 11:6, "But without faith *it is* impossible to please *Him,* for he who comes to God must believe that He is, and *that* He is a rewarder of those who diligently seek Him," Calvary Chapel gives God a chance to work - to venture out in faith - what He wants us to do, not pumping extra energy and effort in a program. In the attitude to venture out in faith, Chuck said, "Let's see if God wants to work today." In Romans 8:31, "What then shall we say to these things? If God *is* for us, who *can be* against us?" we are not afraid to venture in when God wants to be working with us. Take a step in faith. If it works, rejoice. If it doesn't, look for something else. Discover the will of God and then jump into it. Get our heart in harmony with Him, and we will be amazed at what God will do and how God will bless.

<u>My Thought</u>

His thought regarding the balance between the teaching of the Word of God and an open heart to the work of the Holy Spirit impacts on this book's title, "The Spirit Led™ the Life: In the Whole Counsel of God," as Jesus says in John 4:23-24, "But the hour is coming, and now is, when the true worshipers will worship the Father in spirit and truth; for the Father is seeking such to worship Him. [24] God *is* Spirit, and those who worship Him must worship in spirit and truth" and Jesus prays for disciples in John 17:17 "Sanctify them by Your truth. Your word is truth." The balance makes Calvary Chapel Movement distinct, unique, and different from the other churches, so that we have been experiencing and enjoying the balance in His ministry. As long as ministers, missionaries, evangelists, facilitators, the Bible teachers, preachers, elders, or pastors totally depend upon the Holy Spirit, God's purpose shall be effectuated through this theocracy in the body of Christ whose head is Jesus Christ, neither by a man-made-organization based upon democracy, bureaucracy, monarchy, commercialism, or popularism, nor by pumping extra energy, efforts in a program, and raising fund.

In building a church, we sometimes think of a church building, where it is seen that a strife or division occurs in the church because we do not reach expected offerings made by the church members enough to make every monthly payment to a lender or landlord for the building, either a mortgage loan payment or a rental fee.   As Jesus promises in Matthew 6:33 "But seek first the kingdom of God and His righteousness, and all these things (all necessity) shall be added to you," the necessity things are given by the Lord when we seek first His kingdom and righteousness. Then, we can count the given things, not sought things, which is sort of passive faith, for a ministry to the Lord in light of Luke 14:28-30, "For which of you, intending to build a tower, does not sit down first and count the cost, whether he has *enough* to finish *it*— [29] lest, after he has laid the foundation, and is not able to finish, all who see *it* begin to mock him, [30] saying, 'This man began to build and was not able to finish'?" However, rather than we pray to the Lord to resolve the payments and to lead us in His way and we wait patiently on the Lord, we are sometimes tempted to deliver a sermon to raise fund and to develop many ways to raise fund (e.g. invoking competition among church members to make more offerings – many types of offerings, donors' names announced, guest speakers to solicit funds). Then, although the church begins to seek the Kingdom of God, it is flip-flopped that the church is in fact seeking for money to make the payment, becoming a mammon seeker rather than a divine kingdom seeker. The church is no longer dependent upon the power of the Holy Spirit rather than upon the power of mammon. The church is no longer governed by God but the church is a commercial business entity governed by people just like the aforementioned McChurch or the Church of Laodiceans at the last day in Revelation 3:16-17,"So then, because you are lukewarm, and neither cold nor hot, I will vomit you out of My mouth. [17] Because you say, 'I am rich, have become wealthy, and have need of nothing'—and do not know that you are wretched, miserable, poor, blind, and naked."

What are spiritually discerned at the Word of God? First, we in result serve mammon (money god), not God, in Matthew 6:24, "No one can serve two masters; for either he will hate the one and love the other, or else he will be loyal to the one and despise the other. You cannot serve God and mammon."   Second, we also are not within the purpose of an earthly authority ordained by God in Romans 13:1-2, "Let every soul be subject to the governing authorities. For there is no authority except from God, and the authorities that exist are appointed by God. [2] Therefore whoever resists the authority resists the ordinance of God, and those who resist will bring judgment on themselves."   Under relevant laws in the United States, the church is a non-profit corporation.   The church is an artificial person (corporation) to seek not for profit – not for money but for a specific purpose, here a religious purpose in the laws.   The entities for profit are a corporation, a partnership, and a sole proprietary, which are seeking for profits. If they had no profits, they would be closed. However, the non-profit corporation is specially categorized for the purposes of a religion, education, or scientific research and so is tax exempted because "no profit" is "no tax." Therefore, the church seeking for money is not only contrary to God's word but also outside of the purpose of earthly authority (e.g., authority stated in the bylaws of Appendix 2, "a California Non-Profit Religious Corporation.")   Third, is "no money" "no ministry?"   Never because (1) we are content in whatever state, even no money state, in Philippians 4:11 "Not that I speak in regard to need, for I have learned in whatever state I am, to be content:" and (2) our sufficiency is from God, not from money, in 2

Corinthians 3:5, "Not that we are sufficient of ourselves to think of anything as *being* from ourselves, but our sufficiency *is* from God." I feel compassion upon some ministers who become factual mammon seekers in either local churches or foreign missions because they are so stressed to keep the members "coming and giving" for the McChurch or Big Mission. Material or temporary things as means merely exist for the object of spiritual or eternal things. As long as we seek His kingdom and righteousness, all necessary things including our daily bread shall be added by our Lord who is asking us not to worry about them in Matthew 6:24-34.

Also, we sometimes misunderstand that a church is a building rather than a group of Christians. The building is a mere place for our meeting of prayers, worship, the Bible study, fellowship and any other services. The object of the church is born-again Christians (people, not a building) and her means to meet is the building. The place of meeting can be wherever is available, e.g., home, a school, a park, a restaurant, a class room, and so on. So, it is not necessary to be overburdened to make the present payment for the building because the church ministry is not our own ministry based upon own ambitions, own desires, and own wills but His ministry based upon His desires conformed by the Holy Spirit and the Word of God. Insufficient cheerful or willing offerings made by the church members, His sheep, are allowed by our Lord. The growth of the Church stated in the Bible is irrelevant to our efforts. A pastor pasturing over three thousand church members was disqualified because he taught another gospel and it was neither insufficient numbers of church nor insufficient dollars of bank account. The daily addition to the church in Acts 2:47 is His work. Likewise, the willing and cheerful offerings made by His sheep are within the scope of His work, although we might have financial difficulty and consequently spiritual difficulty as Chuck stated. We should commit to serve His sheep, to the Word of God, and to study the Word of God, so as to show ourselves approved unto God. We are pilgrims on the earth for a heavenly country, an eternal kingdom, in Hebrews 11:13-16,"These all died in faith, not having received the promises, but having seen them afar off were assured of them, embraced *them* and confessed that they were strangers and pilgrims on the earth. [14] For those who say such things declare plainly that they seek a homeland. [15] And truly if they had called to mind that *country* from which they had come out, they would have had opportunity to return. [16] But now they desire a better, that is, a heavenly *country.* Therefore God is not ashamed to be called their God, for He has prepared a city for them." The church as a wife is subject to her husband, Christ, in Ephesians 5:23-25, "Wives, submit to your own husbands, as to the Lord. [23] For the husband is head of the wife, as also Christ is head of the church; and He is the Savior of the body. [24] Therefore, just as the church is subject to Christ, so *let* the wives *be* to their own husbands in everything. [25] Husbands, love your wives, just as Christ also loved the church and gave Himself for her." Therefore, we as the church should understand and obey what God says and the direction of the Holy Spirit, that is, "All Scripture" (2 Timothy 3:16-17, stated above) and "what the Spirit says to the church" (Revelation 2:7, 11, 17, 29 and Revelation 3:6, 13, 22), not money-making strategies. Through the Bible Study and Prayers can we understand and obey Him. Then, we as the church can enjoy peace in 1 Corinthians 14:33, "For God is not *the author* of confusion but of peace, as in all the churches of the saints."

In church life or our personal life, we wonder which way is God's direction. Often 3 factors can be considered – (1) 100 % God's glory; (2) applicable verses in the Bible; (3) open circumstances. First, 100% God's glory, not tainted with any self glories, is for God's direction. In the Lord's Prayer, the glory is forever to the Lord in Matthew 6:13 ".......For Yours is the kingdom and the power and the glory forever...." Watch for hidden own glory covered up with God's glory like Ananias and Sapphira (above, in Acts 5:1-4, "But a certain man named Ananias, with Sapphira his wife, sold a possession. ² And he kept back *part* of the proceeds, his wife also being aware *of it,* and brought a certain part and laid *it* at the apostles' feet. ³ But Peter said, "Ananias, why has Satan filled your heart to lie to the Holy Spirit and keep back *part* of the price of the land for yourself? ⁴ While it remained, was it not your own? And after it was sold, was it not in your own control? Why have you conceived this thing in your heart? You have not lied to men but to God." Second, it is applicable verses in the Bible. We should live by every Word of God as Jesus says in Matthew 4:4 "But He answered and said, "It is written, *'Man shall not live by bread alone, but by every word that proceeds from the mouth of God.'"* For instance, a church member asked a pastor to be a surety for a purchased house. The pastor prayed to the Lord about the issue and then God revealed Proverbs 6:1-2, "My son, if you become surety for your friend, *If* you have shaken hands in pledge for a stranger, ² You are snared by the words of your mouth; You are taken by the words of your mouth." The pastor politely refused to be a surety to the member, for whom the pastor provided a room freely. Third, it is open circumstances. We can walk into an open door, not a shut door as Jesus says in Revelation 3:7-8, "And to the angel of the church in Philadelphia write, 'These things says He who is holy, He who is true, *"He who has the key of David, He who opens and no one shuts, and shuts and no one opens"*: [8] "I know your works. See, I have set before you an open door, and no one can shut it; for you have a little strength, have kept My word, and have not denied My name." For the surety case, a vacant house was allowed to be used by another church member and so the pastor was able to provide a room for the needy member. This door was open. But the pastor was not able to be the surety to guarantee the loaned amount of the house to be bought by the member. That door was shut.

In church matters, we should hear of opinions. But we should discern them at the Bible in the Spirit and speak our responses slowly in James 1:19," So then, my beloved brethren, let every man be swift to hear, slow to speak, slow to wrath." One opinion, which a member suggests and sacrifices somehow – time, labor, or offering – only for God's glory, is likely a direction of God, which we should consider. But another opinion, which he suggests alone but never sacrifices anyhow in any ministry, is unlikely a direction of God, which we should pray for him and we, if necessary, may wrath slowly (e.g. destructive opinion of a ministry) to edify the church.

A venture in faith shows Paul's immediately seeking to go to Macedonia upon divine vision, without prior market or demographic survey, in Acts 16:9-10, "And a vision appeared to Paul in the night. A man of Macedonia stood and pleaded with him, saying, "Come over to Macedonia and help us." [10] Now after he had seen the vision, immediately we sought to go to Macedonia, concluding that the Lord had called us to preach the gospel to them." Take a step in faith. If it works, rejoice. If it doesn't, look for an opened door in Revelation 3:7, "And to the angel of the church in Philadelphia write, 'These things says He who is holy, He who is true, *"He who has the key of David, He who opens and no one shuts, and shuts and no one opens."*

1.Self Questions to Confront:

(1) When I am ministering, whose is the ministry?

(2)What are 4 basic functions of the early church? Who added the Christians to the church?

(3) Is the growth of a biblical church relevant to human efforts?

(4) How have I experienced the Holy Spirit in three kinds?

(5) What does "the whole counsel of God" mean to me?

(6) What does "the whole counsel of God" mean?

(7) Where is my sufficiency?

(8) Who can astound and beat the world?

(9) What is God's supreme desire for me?

(10) How do I know God's direction?

(11) Who is really working in me to venture out in faith?

2.Verses to Meditate:

(1) Acts 2:42, "And they continued steadfastly in the apostles' doctrine and fellowship, in the breaking of bread, and in prayers."

(2) Acts 2:47, "praising God and having favor with all the people. And the Lord added to the church daily those who were being saved."

(3) 2 Corinthians 3:5-6, "Not that we are sufficient of ourselves to think of anything as *being* from ourselves, but our sufficiency *is* from God, [6] who also made us sufficient as ministers of the new covenant, not of the letter but of the Spirit; for the letter kills, but the Spirit gives life."

(7) Second by L.E. Romaine [xi]

After reading "Second" written by L.E. Romaine, who was as assistant pastor at Calvary Chapel of Costa Mesa but passed away or moved into heaven, I believed that God called me, as the second, to follow the Lord Jesus, my master. Before planting the present church, I had been the second to help Pastor Duke Kim and Pastor Chuck Smith (masters), to help up their arms as Aaron and Hur did for Moses. It is the role of the servant.

The second term is explained as the following scriptural verses:

1 Corinthians 12:18, "...every one of them in the body as it has pleased Him." To please God, i.e., glorify God; the second and his master in the Body of Christ have the same relationship as the relationship between Joshua (Second) and Moses in Old Testament or between Timothy (Second) and Paul in New Testament. The second must think, look, and do in the role of the servant, not just to say.

Matthew 6:5, "....not be as the hypocrites are...pray standing in the synagogues..." The second had to do the role of the servant as unto the Lord, not showing up as a hypocrite to his master or the church members.

Philippians 2:19-21, "...I trust in the Lord Jesus to send Timothy shortly unto you...." As the disciple Paul trusted in the Lord Jesus Timothy, the second should be a trustful good comfort whom his master trusts in the Lord Jesus. So, the second should support the things which his master did not cover, straightforwardly led fully by the Holy Spirit. If the second is discouraged in doing so, he needs to encourage by himself in the Lord as the second.

Colossians 3:22-24, "Servants, obey in all things your masters…not with eye service….of heart, fearing God…" To build up His body, the second should obey his master in all things, in heart, fearing God, not pretending anything. What the second says must be matched with what he does.

John 10:11-13, "I am the Good Shepherd: the Good Shepherd gives His life for the sheep. But he that is a hireling, and not the Shepherd…" When anyone is hired to do it by the board or somebody, he would be a hireling.   But the second is called to be delegated to serve His sheep (the congregation members) by Jesus Christ, as He served.

1 Corinthians 1:17, "…to preach the Gospel…" Like the disciple Paul, the second is called to preach and teach the Gospel by God and so God may use what he is for furthering His Kingdom and prospering His people.

1 Corinthians 4:13, "Being defamed, we are…the off-scouring of all things unto this day" Although the second is treated as an off-scouring in the world for God, he feels a wonderful way because God SANDPAPERS his ego.

1 Corinthians 1:27-29, "…God has chosen the foolish things of the world…chosen the weak things of the world…"   God chose the second to be used for His kingdom. Through failures, he has been being flexible,

available, and open to whatever molding God wants to do, which is thankful to God.

Philippians 3:12-14 "...forgetting those things which are behind, and reaching forth...for the prize of the high calling of God in Christ Jesus." Being taught by Jesus Christ and the master, the second is pressing toward the Goal for the Prize of God in Jesus Christ, forgetting those things of what he has done.

Ephesians 5:25-28, "Husbands love your wives, even as Christ also loved the church...So ought men to love their wives as their own bodies." The second as a husband should love his wife as Christ loved the Church. And he loves His sheep as his own body.

John 14:26, "But the Comforter, which is the Holy Ghost...He shall teach you all things..." The Holy Spirit has come to establish the fellowship in the Word of God at not only home but also the church, coming to comfort, to empower and to teach the second all things.

Psalms 138:2, "I will worship....praise Your name for Your loving-kindness and for Your truth..." The second will worship and praise God's name for His loving kindness and for His truth by home Bible study to keep both the one fellowship with God individually and the other fellowship of his family members in His love.

1 Timothy 5:8, "But if any provides not for his own, and specially for those of his own house, he has denied the faith, and is worse that an infidel." As Head in his own house, the second should supply all of the

need of the family including the spiritual, keeping the Bible study and working.

Philippians 4:19, "But my God shall supply all your need according to His riches in glory by Christ Jesus." The second should pray for God's supplication, looking at his family finances. God will guide him how to do.

1 Peter 5:3, "...being examples to the flock" The second should be an example to His sheep at the local church by the Comforter.

James 3:1, "My brethren, be not many masters, knowing that we shall receive the greater condemnation" Because the second represents God, he can be interpreted as a master in the context of this verse and so has great responsibility to teach His Word of God. Therefore, the second should pray for each Bible studying to let the Holy Spirit guide him fully.

1 Peter 5:2-4, "Be shepherds of God's flock that is under your care, serving as overseer not because you must, but because your willing, as God wants you to be; not greedy for money, but eager to serve; not lording it over those entrusted to you, but being examples to the flock. And when the Chief Shepherd appears, you will receive the crown of the glory that will never fade away." The second should not be greedy for money, but eager to serve. The second should not be lord over anyone but be an example of His flock, because at Jesus Christ's coming, he will receive the crown of the glory.

In John 1:41-42 (Simon Peter, Cephas) and Acts 9:27 (Barnabas), God used them to bring people to the Lord. Likewise, God desires today for the second to be about the business of bringing others to the Lord.

1Corinthians 12:22-23, "...much more those members of the body...more feeble, are necessary;...our uncomely parts have more abundant comeliness." All parts including the uncomely parts of the body are arranged by God just as He wanted them to be. As a feeble part of ministry, the second should be arranged to His body like "fixing overflowing bathrooms."

Malachi 1:6-10, "A son honors his father...If then I am the Father... To you priests who despise My name Yet you say, 'I what way have we despised Your name? You offer defiled food on My altar...when you offer the blind as a sacrifice, Is not evil?...will He regard your persons?...Nor will I accept an offering from your hands." The second honors God. When he offers something or serves Him, he should offer the best thing and serve God's people in Jesus' name at his best to please God rather than to please men through the power of the Holy Spirit, not for own profit (hireling – SERVING GOD FOR PROFIT).

Malachi 2:1-3, "And now, O priests, this commandment is for you... to give glory to My name... spread refuse on your faces... one will take you away with it" If the second took God's glory, it would be horrible. So as a second should give the glory to God alone. Otherwise, he would be condemned by God.

Malachi 2:7, "For the lips of a priest...he is the messenger of the Lord of hosts." The second is the messenger of the Lord of hosts. He is someone who takes care of the sheep as GOD DIRECTS.

Acts 2:46-47 "And they continuing daily with one accord in the temple... The Lord added to the church daily such as should be saved" The members of the church will be added daily by Him, not by my efforts. So, the second should look at his heart which is what God concerned about.

Hebrews 4:13, "...all things are naked and opened unto the eyes of Him with whom we have to do" The service of the second is open before Him, so that he should pray for Him before service and he should serve to God and to the church members as he does to God.

Psalms 139:3, "You comprehend my path and my lying down, and are acquainted with all my ways." God knows the second of whether or not his service is either to Him or to Man or for his interest. So, faithfully the second should serve to God through teaching or preaching Gospel to His sheep.

Acts 20:28, "Take heed therefore unto yourselves, and to all the flock, over the which the Holy Ghost has made you overseers, to fee the church of God, which he has purchase with his own blood." The second should take off my speck first, depending upon the Holy Ghost, and faithfully feed the church composed of Christians purchased by His Shed Blood.

For my thought about the personal application to me of the cited scriptures, it means to me to be the second of Jesus Christ to let Him direct and guide me in serving Him and His people for His glory. I have the heart to follow whatever He desires, through being led fully and flexibly by the Holy Spirit in the Word of God. Let Christ be increasing, but keep myself decreasing. I may let Him get the credit for the work, which I have done, because the Holy Spirit leads me over my life. To be a Pastor of Calvary Chapel of Anaheim Hills international church is to be a Second of Christ.

A "master" named by Romaine is called as a "mentor" by Hendricks in the book of "As Iron Sharpens Iron,[xii]" in proverbs 27:17," As iron sharpens iron, So a man sharpens the countenance of his friend." For our Lord Jesus Christ, Romaine is for the second or the mentored person who is humbly assisting his master or mentor and whose characteristics are described in the Bible, while Hendricks are for the mentor or the master who is influencing, affecting, and impacting on the second to multiply ministries and whose characteristics are described. Although both terms of the "mentor" and "the second" are not stated in the Bible, I got impressed with both books and personally use both terms favorably and practice within the zone of the Bible for the Kingdom of God.

1.Self Questions to Confront:

(1) What do "the second" and "the mentor" mean? What is the difference between a hireling and the second?

(2) Who sandpapers my ego?

2.Verses to Meditate:

(1) Colossians 3:22-24,"Bondservants, obey in all things your masters according to the flesh, not with eye-service, as men-pleasers, but in sincerity of heart, fearing God. [23] And whatever you do, do it heartily, as to the Lord and not to men, [24] knowing that from the Lord you will receive the reward of the inheritance; for you serve the Lord Christ."

> (2) 1 Corinthians 4:13 "being defamed, we entreat. We have been made as the filth of the world, the off-scouring of all things until now.
>
> (3) Proverbs 27:17," *As* iron sharpens iron, So a man sharpens the countenance of his friend."

Videos:

(1) A Venture in Faith [xiii]

In the video of "Venture in Faith," explained above as "venture out in faith," God worked from beginning. God had plans, making instruments to be complete. Pentecost experiences to focus on Jesus Christ. After healing Chuck's sister, Chuck was born. He began to memorize the Word of God. His mother's praying day and night impacted Chuck's Christian life. He originally had desire to go to medical school, but he had more challenged to save people to eternity. He went to a Bible college. He took courses sincerely and took extra courses at the Biola University. Dr. Guy Duffleid and Dr. Nico, the teachers of the Bible College, said that "Chuck is a good student." After marriage with Kay, he served to Arizona church and Corona in California while walking in a grocery to provide to family. Hippie people were accepted to Huntington Beach Church in 1960. It is called, "Calvary Chapel movement." The movement accepted abandoned people, applied the Word of God practically, did not allege denomination, supported the Work of the Holy Spirit.

Where God Guide

The forty five dollars ($45) per month rental fee were paid by Chuck, who earned fifteen dollars ($15) per week. Today, church has a problem of the large building payment but of little expense to feed sheep. But Chuck learned in the hard living experience as to how to live simply to provide the need for him. Dr. Hocking supported Chuck, stating that in the Calvary Chapel movement people had total dependence upon God. Simplicity in dependence upon God is an important factor of the movement. Ministry stands for Service. It is to serve to people, not to be served by the people. God really provides a real minister with the need. The minister is not a psychological teacher but a teacher of the Word of God who recognizes God. Through all the ways, God initiated Chuck who responded to God's direction. To flatter man is meaningless.

Children Ministry

Frustration of ministry came from a man's leading rather than God's leading. In Ephesians 4:11, ministers are equippers to make people to edify the body of Christ. Ministers reveal the full knowledge of God to people to be healthy sheep. Teaching the Whole Scripture within the Scripture in the context leads to verse by verse expository teaching. It did not use mimic but uses the Scripture. Living Word and Working Word and Powerful Word are in the Scripture.

Hippie Movement

Upon Ephesians 4:11-16, "[11] And He Himself gave some *to be* apostles, some prophets, some evangelists, and some pastors and teachers, [12] for the equipping of the saints for the work of ministry, for the edifying of the body of Christ, [13] till we all come to the unity of the faith and of the knowledge of the Son of God, to a perfect man, to the measure of the stature of the fullness of Christ; [14] that we should no longer be children, tossed to and fro and carried about with every wind of doctrine, by the trickery of men, in the cunning craftiness of deceitful plotting, [15] but, speaking the truth in love, may grow up in all things into Him who is the head—Christ— [16] from whom the whole body, joined and knit together by what every joint supplies, according to the effective working by which every part does its share, causes growth of the body for the edifying of itself in love," Chuck had a desire to be an independent church from any denomination who frustrated God's direction, planting a Calvary Chapel composed of 25 people. Chuck fully trusted God to lead the church. Then a lot of sheep added and fed were prophesized. Chuck waited and saw God's work as to very strong home fellowship through human contacts and worship to God at home. In Romans 10:17, "So then faith *comes* by hearing, and hearing by the Word of God," hearing from the Word of God changed the people's lives. Chuck completed the Scripture for 2 years. The 1960 Hippie movement, many young people left from home and wore casual clothes and left from a well-organized tradition. The Lord took them and led them some way. Chuck believed that Church was open to any kinds of people. The early church in the book of Acts was directed by the Holy Spirit.

A New Worship Style

A new worship style was developed with atmosphere of worship, flexible worship, and music song, led by the Holy Spirit. Same truth has been communicated with what types of music – hymn, contemporary music, rock music or country songs.   The point is to get people going to Cross. Dr. John McArthur said, "Focus on Gospel regardless of style."

A Living Theology

Gospel is living everyday regardless of culture, style, or racial colors. Several people   characterized the theology of Calvary Chapel with "teaching of the Word of God," "Inspiration of Worship," "No rules or programs," "Every common people coming into the Calvary Chapel," "General Openness,"   "Flexible," "Not broken,"   "Very Casual Approach," "Equipping Christians rather than Evangelism," "Feed the body and so the evangelism is the byproduct of the body," "More Bible studying," and "More people coming to Christ and consequently their helping the homeless and resolving the social issues as well." Wherever we go, we are doing service or ministering, i.e., apply faith wherever we go.

A Balanced Theology

We keep the balance among grace, salvation, and the work of the Holy Spirit. Pieces of the balanced theology are the oldest evangelical doctrine which is to cleanse sins, the power of the Holy Spirit, and the fulfillment of prophecy. The openness to the gift of the Holy Spirit is the Healthy Charismatic movement which is not a charismatic church but which is belief in the validity of gifts of the Holy Spirit, verified by the Word of God. For the works of gifts of the Holy Spirit, we keep the balance between teaching the Word of God and the Holy Spirit's works, experiencing in sign which is verified by the word.   But the strong body is being built up with the Love of Christ, rather important than any differences, and with Grace of our Lord.

A Unique Leadership Style

Chuck Smith rolled up all trash, being an example before the other Christians. He always looked at people's opportunity and witnesses with heart, openness and flexibility to God. The discipleship observes him who is the model. Freedom is given to all pastors because let them be guided by God as well as let them be responsible to God, but he is conservative in finance. Message is relevant to the congregation, not to a big Ivy Tower. Don't take ministers seriously because God takes care of them. He has soft Charisma from the members of Church and the spiritual commitment. There is not power of individual but power of God.

The Future of Calvary Chapel

Hippie was changed to Yuppie. Now the ministry is to Yuppie. One is a danger to institutionalize. We can keep with the same heart as Chuck, "Christ's love constraints me." As long as we love Christ and keep faithful toward God, the danger to institutionalize will be gone away because we are praying, studying the Word of God, and walk in the power of the Holy Spirit. Not based upon the dollars of bank account or numbers of church. Women, money, and human glory destroy a ministry and so we spend more time in prayer rather than personal communication or participation in seminary. Regardless of agreement or disagreement, we focus on mutual love, teaching/preaching the Word of God, experiences verified by the Word, and building up the Body.

Chuck Smith

He reveals God's love, depends upon God, is humble, is silent, is very easy to talk, walks by God's power, stands in integrity which is a man of God (not superman), and is filling up the emptiness of people. We are acknowledging God, are touching the body whose head is Jesus Christ, are looking to the future with the priority of the Word of God, and are working in different ministries.

My Thought

After watching the video of "a venture in faith," Calvary Chapel movement emphasized the balance between the teaching of the Word of God and an open heart to the work of the Holy Spirit, disregarding human efforts, e.g., (1) the programs of the Bible College or the School of Ministry not being sought for an Accreditation, that might control the contents of studies rather than that submit to the Words of God. In Romans 1:26-27, "For this reason God gave them up to vile passions. For even their women exchanged the natural use for what is against nature. [27] Likewise also the men, leaving the natural use of the woman, burned in their lust for one another, men with men committing what is shameful, and receiving in themselves the penalty of their error which was due," homosexual is considered as sin that should be repented to the Lord rather than considered as a disadvantage person who should be treated equally under a law in the World, In 1 Timothy 2:12-14, "And I do not permit a woman to teach or to have authority over a man, but to be in silence. [13] For Adam was formed first, then Eve. [14] And Adam was not deceived, but the woman being deceived, fell into transgression," no ordination to a woman as pastor might be deemed as gender discrimination under a worldly law. We obey worldly laws unless the laws are conflict with the Word of God, in Romans 13:1 "Let every soul be subject to the governing authorities. For there is no authority except from God, and the authorities that exist are appointed by God," and in Acts 5:29, "But Peter and the *other* apostles answered and said: "We ought to obey God rather than men." (2) The mostly efficient way to teach the "Whole" counsel of God is verse by verse, chapter by chapter, book by book inductive expository teaching the entire Bible, not opposing deductive or topical teaching unless a pastor or teacher's thought might distort God's thought in the context of the Bible.

Freedom is given to us with all other pastors because let us be guided freely by God as well as let us be responsible to God. With Christ's heart, we are also conservative in finance according to the Bible. In 2 Corinthians 8:12, "For if there is first a willing mind, *it is* accepted according to what one has, *and* not according to what he does not have," members' willing offerings are accepted to the Lord, not published in any form but every quarterly finance reports are made in total offerings and 4 areas expenses of (1) taking care expense of Sheep in Galatians 6:6," Let him who is taught the word share in all good things with him who teaches," (2) Delivering Gospel Expense in Philippians 4:15-19,"Now you Philippians know also that in the beginning of the gospel, when I departed from Macedonia, no church shared with me concerning giving and receiving but you only. [16] For even in Thessalonica you sent *aid* once and again for my necessities. [17] Not that I seek the gift, but I seek the fruit that abounds to your account. [18] Indeed I have all and abound. I am full, having received from Epaphroditus the things *sent* from you, a sweet-smelling aroma, an acceptable sacrifice, well pleasing to God. [19] And my God shall supply all your need according to His riches in glory by Christ Jesus." (3) Charity Expense in Matthew 25:40, "And the King will answer and say to them, 'Assuredly, I say to you, inasmuch as you did *it* to one of the least of these My brethren, you did *it* to Me.'" and (4) Minister Reward Expense in 1 Timothy 5:17-18, "Let the elders who rule well be counted worthy of double honor, especially those who labor in the word and doctrine. [18] For the Scripture says, *"You shall not muzzle an ox while it treads out the grain,"* and, "The laborer *is* worthy of his wages." Sometimes whether or not tithe is expired in the New Testament is raised up. We in a conservative way understand and practice the tithe with the willing mind in 2 Corinthians 8:12. In Matthew 23, Jesus taught to the multitude and to His disciples (23:1) and in verse 23, "Woe to you, scribes and Pharisees, hypocrites! For you pay tithe of mint and anise and cummin, and have neglected the weightier *matters* of the law: justice and mercy and faith. These you ought to have done, without leaving the others undone." Jesus recommends, "ought to," that based upon justice, mercy, and faith we should do tithe. In Luke 11:42, "But woe to you Pharisees! For you tithe mint and rue and all manner of herbs, and pass by justice and the love of God. These you ought to have done, without leaving the others undone," it is taught that we as His disciples with justice and the love of God should do tithe. Here is also the tithe recommended, not the mandatory tithe of the Old Testament in Malachi 3:8, "Will a man rob God? Yet you have robbed Me! But you say, 'In what way have we robbed You?' In tithes and offerings." So, we never ask forced tithe and offering but recommend willing and cheerful tithe and offering because we're bought with the price of Jesus' blood shed and belong to Him and so really anything and everything is His in 1 Corinthians 3:23, "And you *are* Christ's, and Christ *is* God's," and we love Him more than anything else.

A big Ivy tower, institutionalization, and 3 G (abbreviated girl, gold and glory) are destroyers to ministries, because, first, a big ivy tower that exalts itself against the Word of God should be cast down but be brought into captivity to the obedience of God. Otherwise, the big ivy tower would destroy our simply teaching the simple Word of God relevant to the congregation in the Spirit. Second, the institutionalization for the dollars of bank account and numbers of church would destroy our praying, studying the Word of God, and walking in the power of the Holy Spirit. Third, sinless Jesus' example for temptations in part of a man in Matthew 4:1-11 and in Luke 4:1-13 shows woman, money, and human glory (girl, gold, and glory, called as "3 G") leads focus on others than God (e.g. adulterous heart rather than pure heart, focus on earth rather than focus on heaven, man's center rather than God's center, pride rather than thanksgiving to the Lord for our given favors), destroying ministries. Therefore, we focus on prayer to seek God's will, mutual love, preaching and teaching the Word of God, life experiences verified by the Word, and building up the Body of Christ.

When I listened to the message of Chuck, hospitalized after he got two minor strokes, through network, he exposed Joseph's story in Genesis as any connected happenings in God's control (discussed above in the preface), reflecting his full trust in the Lord and conforming this video of "A venture in Faith."   On my life experiences at several denominational churches, I believe and experience that the Calvary Chapel non-denominational movement is the most way close to God's way by saying "Led by the Holy Spirit," "Grace changes everything," "Let go, let God," "Trust in the Lord with all your heart," "Whose Church?," and "The Whole Counsel of God."

1.Self Questions to Confront:

(1) How much should I depend upon God during my life?

(2) Why can I frustrate a ministry?

(3) What is difference between Charismatic movement and Charismatic church?

(4) Who is my initiator to live?

(5) Do I apply faith wherever I go?

(6) Am I given freedom by whom? To whom am I responsible?

(7) What destroy my ministry to the Lord?

2.Verses to Meditate:

(1) John 8:32 "And you shall know the truth, and the truth shall make you free."

(2) 1 John 2:16, "For all that *is* in the world—the lust of the flesh, the lust of the eyes, and the pride of life—is not of the Father but is of the world"

---

(2) How and Why Series by Chuck Smith [xiv]

"How And Why" video which teaches to pastors to deal normal functions in local churches of Calvary Chapel taught by Chuck Smith is recorded on three (3) parts of video.

First part of "How" are (1) Church Dedication and (2) Communion Service. Second part of "And" is (1) Baptism, (2) Marriage, and (3) Baby Dedication. And the last third part of "Why" is "The Memorial Service."

How

Church Dedication

It is our dedication of the facility, which is the place to meet together, to God the Farther in eternal prospective, although God exists everywhere. We saw Solomon's dedication service in 1 Kings 8:22-66 and in verse 63, "And Solomon offered a sacrifice of peace offerings, which he offered to the LORD, twenty-two thousand bulls and one hundred and twenty thousand sheep. So the king and all the children of Israel dedicated the house of the LORD." In the service, many people such as general contractor, subcontractor, city counsel, city people, and new face people came to participate. They were given opportunity to see new facility and to get Gospel.

Chuck taught the church dedication of Calvary Chapel of Santa Barbara being served by Pastor Rick Ryan. In Samuel, although Israelites were surrounded by Philistines, Lord set up us to defeat them. Likewise, Lord set up us the facility to complete, although it was not still completed yet. David just had the desire to build up the temple, although there was neither material nor budget. But Solomon completed the facility because God gave him more than enough. In Psalm 73, we often wondered because of the circumstances that we did not understand although we knew that surely Lord is good, loves us, and controls the circumstances of our lives. Then, we see a big picture in eternal prospective, not focusing on a little piece of happening like a puzzle game. God sees our whole pictures for eternal plan. In verse 12 and 13, Satan used our physical weakness, attaching emotionally (feel no good) and spiritually (God doesn't love you, really?). Often Satan generalized or exaggerated beyond particular facts. Misinterpretation misled to wrong conclusion. We were painful until we are in sanctuary of God. There we cleanse all iniquity, unfairness, confusion, or misunderstanding, and we have new life or divine prospective or eternal prospective. This is the purpose of facility.

<u>Communion Service</u>

It is a memorial service to remind us the past event of death of Jesus Christ, in light of suffering, love, and sin. Traditionally, we have communion service the first Sunday or every Sunday. Scripture says "often" communion service but it does not tell in particular.

After worship team's songs, Chuck taught. Israelites memorized them to be delivered from Egypt slavery bondage by God in the feast of Passover. The feast of tabernacle reminded them to God's preservation for 40 years in wilderness. Likewise, the communion service reminds us to Jesus' death for our sins, God's love to give us only begotten son, restoration of fellowship with God. And Chuck read Luke 23. Then, first, while bread was served to Congregational members, worship team sang songs. After Chuck's prayer, they took it together. Second, while cup was served to the members, worship team sang songs. After Chuck's prayer, they took it together. Communion service is memorial service of Jesus' death in light of love (bread - body) and redemption of sin (cup – blood).

And

Baptism

Water baptism is publicly acknowledged that old life is dead and new life is born again. Old life following after flesh was deleted and new life following Jesus Christ begins. We walk in spirit. We have fellowship with Jesus. Water means "Grave." When we merged into water, we died into the grave. During merging in water, our old life was wasted. When we went out of water, we rose again after spirit. We are born again for God's pleasure, not for our flesh's pleasure. But we need a food continuously. This is a spiritual food, which is the Word of God. First, to feed up is first "Learn to Me (I will give you rest or peace)," second "Take My yoke upon you (let Me direct your life)," and third "Lean of Me (know My love, My plan of your life for God's purpose). After accepting the Lord Jesus heartily, you are encouraged to get water baptism publicly, and then to read the Bible.

Marriage (Weddings)

Marriage is ordained by God. It is the important time to have relationship of Couple. The problem of the marriage is marriage with unbeliever, which is unequally yoke relationship. Two golden rules are (1) husband, love wife, as Christ gave His life for church (Ephesians 5:25), and (2) wife, submit yourself to husband as to Lord (Ephesians 5:22).

Weddings are both come side by side before God to join husband and wife. Marriage is ordained by God; both are the most intimate relationship as husband and wife. Becoming one flesh, they may become father and mother. It is not good that man lives alone (Genesis 2:18). Chuck asked groom to honor her and bride to honor him. Each declares vow after repeating after Chuck. Then, each exchanges rings symbolizing "eternity, love, and pledge." Chuck prayed them to unite one as husband and wife. Communion service was held to the couple.

<u>Baby Dedication</u>

Infant baptism is not biblical because infants can't decide own decision for their life. In 1 Samuel 1, Hanna dedicated her infant, Samuel, to God all the days of his life, according to His whole purpose in 1 Samuel 1:11, "Then she made a vow and said, "O LORD of hosts, if You will indeed look on the affliction of Your maidservant and remember me, and not forget Your maidservant, but will give Your maidservant a male child, then I will give him to the LORD all the days of his life, and no razor shall come upon his head." Chuck prayed to each child for the baby dedication, "O Lord, we dedicate his (her) life for Your purpose."

Why

<u>The Memorial Service</u>

The memorial service has two aspects – one is memorial and the other is eternity. The service shows joy, blessing, and sorrow.   In the memorial service, funeral service contains (1) the personal history memorized by husband, granddaughter, or friend, etc, and (2) what's future we share the Gospel of Jesus Christ.   Grave service should be short, raising the issue of resurrection.   In the orders of the watched service, there are solo songs, Chuck's prayer, husband's memory of his decedent wife, songs, granddaughter's memory of her, songs, her friend's memory, song, and then Chuck's message – (1) her love and her hospitality, (2) His purpose of her life (love relationship with God necessary), (3) death – two meanings (one is the physical death - the separation of the consciousness from the body or the separation of spirit from your body and the other is the spiritual death, the separation of man's consciousness from God, e.g., physical life only for his pleasure but his spiritual death), (4) Her earthly tent went into dust but she moved in beautiful mansion (2 Corinthians 5:1)   and God prepares for new glorified body in her resurrection, and (5) our hope of eternal life in Jesus, glory reunion, eternity kingdom, and resurrection with incorruptible body. Chuck prayed and announced for grave side service.

<u>My Thought</u>

It's very helpful for me to deal normal function in Calvary Chapel of Anaheim Hills, especially, a congressional member's baptism at Dona

Point Beach and a memorial service at Moreno Valley. I am impressed with the baptism and the memorial service that were very natural way. Chuck and baptized persons never wore any white gowns but wore normal suits at Corona Delma Beach. Each born again Christian willingly joined in the baptism ceremony before the public, following Jesus' baptism ceremony. If a baptism ceremony itself were pre-requirement for the salvation, the baptism ceremony human work would be added to faith for the salvation. Equally, the baptism of a baby (e.g. the infant baptism for my children had done so before joining in the Calvary Chapel) who by himself is not able to understand the salvation Gospel and so is not able to believe except his parents' effort to bring is not accepted. However, a baby dedication to the Lord is accepted in Luke 2:22-23, "Now when the days of her purification according to the law of Moses were completed, they brought Him to Jerusalem to present *Him* to the Lord [23] (as it is written in the law of the Lord, *"Every male who opens the womb shall be called holy to the LORD")*."

The memorial services were also very natural way. After relative's and friend's presenting memories of the decedent, Chuck naturally gave hope and blessing messages, without rigid formality as I have done so in several memorial services so far. The communion service at every 1st week Sunday worship service, or at wedding ceremony, remembers us of Jesus' death for us, in light of love (bread-body) and redemption of sin (cup-blood) in 1 Corinthians 11:23-26, "For I received from the Lord that which I also delivered to you: that the Lord Jesus on the *same* night in which He was betrayed took bread; [24] and when He had given thanks, He broke *it* and said, "Take, eat; this is My body which is broken for you; do this in remembrance of Me." [25] In the same manner *He* also *took* the cup after supper, saying, "This cup is the new covenant in My blood. This do, as often as you drink *it,* in remembrance of Me." [26] For as often as you eat this bread and drink this cup, you proclaim the Lord's death till He comes."

The thoughts of books, videos, or lectures make us to understand faithfully the Bible, filling my thirst for the Bible during my life.

1.Self Questions to Confront:

(1) Did I participate in Church dedication, communion service, water baptism, wedding service, and/or baby dedication?

(2) Does God see my whole picture for eternal plan?

(3) What does communion service mean to me?

(4) What does Christ's saying to "Take My yoke upon you" mean to me?

(5) In the wedding what does "the exchange of rings" mean to the couples?

(6) What are two aspects that the memorial service has?

(7) What are two types of death?

(8) When can I have a water baptism ceremony before the public?

2.Verses to Meditate:

(1) Luke 2:22-23, "Now when the days of her purification according to the law of Moses were completed, they brought Him to Jerusalem to present *Him* to the Lord [23] (as it is written in the law of the Lord, *"Every male who opens the womb shall be called holy to the LORD")"*

(2) 1 Corinthians 11:23-26, "For I received from the Lord that which I also delivered to you: that the Lord Jesus on the *same* night in which He

was betrayed took bread; [24] and when He had given thanks, He broke *it* and said, "Take, eat; this is My body which is broken for you; do this in remembrance of Me." [25] In the same manner *He* also *took* the cup after supper, saying, "This cup is the new covenant in My blood. This do, as often as you drink *it,* in remembrance of Me." [26] For as often as you eat this bread and drink this cup, you proclaim the Lord's death till He comes."

Cast Down Thoughts?

God says in Colossians 2:8 "Beware lest anyone cheat you through philosophy and empty deceit, according to the tradition of men, according to the basic principles of the world, and not according to Christ." Any thoughts against the knowledge of God or Christ should be cast down (in 2 Corinthians 10:5, above) to be discerned by "….the sword of the Spirit, which is the Word of God (Ephesians 6:17), "God's knowledge should not be put in a man's frame because a finite man has a limited understanding to infinite God's knowledge, even if you don't understand as Peter teaches in 2 Peter 3:16, "as also in all his epistles, speaking in them of these things, in which are some things hard to understand, which untaught and unstable *people* twist to their own destruction, as *they do* also the rest of the Scriptures."

For preaching, from the cast down thoughts we may develop parables close to hearers' thoughts with the Agape love of Jesus who gave everything for us. Some cast down thoughts I experienced were above discussed in the preface.

1. "Christian's devil possession" – should be cast down because Christians are the temple of the living God, never able to be possessed by demon in 2 Corinthians 6:14-16, "Do not be unequally yoked together with unbelievers. For what fellowship has righteousness with lawlessness? And what communion has light with darkness? [15] And what accord has Christ with Belial? Or what part has a believer with an unbeliever? [16] And what agreement has the temple of God with idols? For you are the temple of the living God. As God has said."   As stated above in the preface, this is the answer to his prayer for "Go out, a cold devil" to me who was a born-again Christian.

2. "The Word Faith movement" [xv]is also known as the Word of Faith. Whatever a believer wants and prays constantly, God will provide it. A believer uses God, rather than God uses a believer for divine purpose. The believer is the master or the Lord but God is a mere assistant for human purpose. The Word Faith movement should be cast down because its initiator is a man. In the preface, my "consistent prayer to be admitted by the college" regardless of initial God's will is a typical example of this faith movement, which I repented after Chuck's teaching. Initiator must be God in Romans 8:14, "For as many as are led by the Spirit of God, these are sons of God." Thus, we are always respondents to Him and we enjoy the Spirit led life. In the same reason, "purpose driven life" or "positive thought" should be

accepted in part only if the purpose or the positive thought comes from God, not from man, while the above taught "Venture in Faith" is accepted. The Word Faith movement is often practiced with the prosperity gospel (Below).

3. "Prosperity Gospel" doctrine [xvi]is the gospel that God provides His children material prosperity, wealth and physical health. It should be rejected because all believers in the Bible were not prosperous during their physical life. Paul's physical weakness is shown in Galatians 4:13, "You know that because of physical infirmity I preached the gospel to you at the first." Jesus Himself was dead on cross in John 19:30 "So when Jesus had received the sour wine, He said, "It is finished!" And bowing His head, He gave up His spirit." In the answer of the sermon in "3 John 1:2" stated above in the preface, John the elder says to Gaius, "Beloved, I pray that you may prosper in all things and be in health, just as your soul prospers." Pray (proseukomai, the Greek word) is often misinterpreted with God's promise (epangelomai, the Greek word) for the prosperity gospel doctrine. We as the children of God may pray for material prosperity (here, "all things" and "health") to our heavenly Father, beyond soul and/or spiritual prosperity, but He will determine to give the material prosperity in His time, not our time. For the Beatitudes in Matthew 5:1-12, they also misunderstood "blessed (makalois, the Greek word)" as "material blessing" in stead of "exceeding glad" taught by Jesus in Matthew 5:12. This doctrine tends to the life driven by man's efforts, for the purpose of the material prosperity, rather than the life led by the Spirit.

4. "Positive Thought" doctrine is the doctrine to think of no matter what in a positive way. The conforming factor in the image of Christ for our Christian life is not our positive thought but the Word of God in the Spirit. The Word of God includes not only positive thought but also negative thought. For example, 1 Thessalonians 5:16 says "Rejoice always" positively while Luke 9:23 says "Then He said to *them* all, "If anyone desires to come after Me, let him deny himself, and take up his cross daily, and follow Me" for self denial, negatively. Jesus compares between the sheep and the goats in Matthew 25:40-41, "And the King will answer and say to them, 'Assuredly, I say to you, inasmuch as you did *it* to one of the least of these My brethren, you did *it* to Me.' (in positive thought for reward)[41] "Then He will also say to those on the left hand, 'Depart from Me, you cursed, into the everlasting fire prepared for the devil and his angels" (in negative thought for eternal judgment). The discerner for our thought is not our positive thought but the Word of God itself in Hebrews 4:12, "For the Word of God *is* living and powerful, and sharper than any two-edged sword, piercing even to the division of soul and spirit, and of joints and marrow, and is a discerner of the thoughts and intents of the heart." Therefore, this doctrine undermines the Whole Counsel of God.

5. "Feeling Good" doctrine dominates teaching and preaching to make hearers feel good such as "love," "joy," "peace," "comfort," "hope," "blessing," "mercy," "grace," "prosperity," "eternal life," "victory," and so on. But the doctrine negates "patience," "long

suffering," "persecution," "judgment," "righteousness," "faithfulness," "humility," "many tears," and so on. Therefore, this doctrine pleases men, not God, in Galatians 1:10, "For do I now persuade men, or God? Or do I seek to please men? For if I still pleased men, I would not be a bondservant of Christ." This doctrine like the positive thought doctrine undermines the Whole Counsel of God.

6. "The Toronto blessing" movement[xvii][xviii] is also known as "holy laughter ministry," "new wave of the Holy Spirit," "Vineyard movement," "High Voltage Christianity," or "Signs and wonders movement." They are based on tongues, extreme feeling, healing, meeting a dead person, holy laughing, roaring in the spirit, extraordinary feelings, Yoga power, and peace coming from such experiences, which were allegedly "grace gifts" given by the Holy Spirit, rather than manifested on the Word of God, i.e., not in "the whole counsel of God." These are simply extra-biblical experiences, although they alleged constantly "the power of God" because they were uncontrolled with holy laughing, shaking, or falling based upon the vibration of God. Some part is biblical such as a gift of the Holy Spirit – tongue and healing in 1 Corinthians 12:9-10, "to another faith by the same Spirit, to another gifts of healings by the same Spirit, to another the working of miracles, to another prophecy, to another discerning of spirits, to another *different* kinds of tongues, to another the interpretation of tongues" – but the other most parts of laughing, shaking, falling, transferring conducts, meeting dead person, extreme feeling, etc are not found in any scripture. For

example, "holy laughter," in Genesis 21:6 "And Sarah said, "God has made me laugh, *and* all who hear will laugh with me," in the context of the Bible, no such biblical basis of "holy laughter" is found rather than the interpretation of their own heart in Jeremiah 23:16 "Thus says the LORD of hosts: "Do not listen to the words of the prophets who prophesy to you. They make you worthless; They speak a vision of their own heart, Not from the mouth of the LORD." Therefore, the movement is mostly based on "extra-biblical experiences," "non-scriptural experiences," "emotional experiences," or "soulish experiences irrelevant to spiritual experiences," as discussed in part in the preface, and so most parts inconsistent with the Bible should be rejected.

7. Living Stream Ministry (LSM)[xix] published the Recovery Version of the Bible. LSM was established by Witness Lee. He promotes Watchman Nee,[xx] imprisoned in 1952 for his faith and dead in 1972, who wrote "The Normal Christian Life[xxi]" about "Christian Living" in light of the Book of Romans. LSM's spiritual revival from the Bible is discerned at the Bible to be accepted, but   the authority tainted from Confucianism (e.g. coercive leader, previously discussed in the preface) is different from the Bible, because the leader stated in the Bible are a servant leader in Matthew 20:28, "just as the Son of Man did not come to be served, but to serve, and to give His life a ransom for many" and Matthew 23:11, "But he who is greatest among you shall be your servant," e.g. pastor picking up trash who was thrown away by his Sheep. No coercive leader, coming from Confucianism, is stated in the Bible. Therefore, the authority tainted from

Confucianism is discerned simply not to be accepted, without any judgmental word of "cult" or "heresy" because God says in James 4:12 "There is one Lawgiver, who is able to save and to destroy. Who are you to judge another?"

Their strong opposition of denominational churches due to division of the unity of Christ is understandable. After conversion to the Christian from the Buddhist, I got struggled in the turmoil of denominations during whole college life (stated above). In church history[xxii], after the early church in the Book of Acts, throughout persecution and King Constantine's declaration of the Christianity as the National Religion in 315 AD, Catholic churches had developed but many impurity (e.g. paganism, politics, indulgence, etc.) came in, being protested and/or reformed by John Wycliffe (1324-1384), Erasmus (1466-1536), Martin Luther (1483-1546), John Calvin (1509-64), John Knox (1515-72), etc. The protest or reformation caused so many denominational churches. The denominations could cause not only (1) unbiblical points to divide the unity of believers in our Lord Jesus Christ in Ephesians 1:22-23, "And He put all *things* under His feet, and gave Him *to be* head over all *things* to the church, [23] which is His body, the fullness of Him who fills all in all.," but also (2) biblical points to minister and act in diversity in 1 Corinthians 12:5-6, "There are differences of ministries, but the same Lord. [6] And there are diversities of activities, but it is the same God who works all in all." In the present Calvary Chapel Anaheim Hills, Christians, who grew up in Methodists, the Salvation Army, Baptists, The Christian and Missionary Alliance

(CMA), Christian Reformed Church(CRC), and Presbyterian Church, have ministered and acted in the unity of Christ and in diversity for His kingdom and His glory, as the model of (1) early church led, filled, and empowered by the Spirit stated in the Book of Acts, before historically Catholic church or Protestants occurrence, and of (2) the Philadelphia church, as a last church, stated by Jesus in Revelation 3:8, "......you have a little strength, have kept My word, and have not denied My name," showing that the decisive factor is whether or not each has "The Spirit Led Life in the Whole Counsel of God" rather than whether or not each belonged to which denomination.

Therefore, their strong opposition of denominational churches due to division of the unity of Christ is different from us who do not oppose them only except their over emphasis of doctrinal differences that have led to the division of the body of Christ although we are a non-denominational church. But we believe that the only true basis of Christian fellowship is His Agape love, which is greater than any differences we possess and without which we have no right to claim ourselves Christians.

8. Seventh-day Adventists[xxiii] – known as "Adventists." They believe in Trinity and infallible Bible and Jesus' 2nd coming as other biblical churches, distinctive with only Saturday service and food strictly literal application by the Old Testament, unconscious state of the dead, and the doctrine of an investigative judgment, etc. Trinity, infallible Bible, and Jesus' 2nd coming come from the Bible (discussed below in the Faith Statement) but only

Saturday service and food strictly literal application by the Old Testament is not accepted because the strictness may be one way to the Christian who wants to do so, not only way, and in the Whole counsel of God, Jesus - at His disciples' plucking the ears of corn on Sabbath day - says in Mark 2: 27, "And He said to them, "The Sabbath was made for man, and not man for the Sabbath." In the same token, for food, Paul says in 1 Corinthians 8:8-9, "But food does not commend us to God; for neither if we eat are we the better, nor if we do not eat are we the worse. 9 But beware lest somehow this liberty of yours become a stumbling block to those who are weak," and so I would not eat pork if a weak Christian who believes in Deuteronomy 14:8, "Also the swine is unclean for you, because it has cloven hooves, yet *does* not *chew* the cud; you shall not eat their flesh or touch their dead carcasses." Otherwise, I would freely enjoy it because I personally love it. Their additional teaching of unconscious state of the dead, and the doctrine of an investigative judgment, etc, is totally not accepted because they are added simply to the Bible.

9. Emerging Church or Emergent church seeks to "deconstruct" the meaning of the Bible and to "reconstruct" the meaning combined with the thoughts of people who live in a postmodern culture or postmodernism, by often communicating with other believers and even atheists[xxiv].   They seek all understood their faith in a postmodern culture in the name of Jesus, undermining the authentic Bible, virgin Birth of Jesus Christ, vicarious death of Jesus Christ for our sins, sufficient work of the Holy Spirit, Bodily resurrection (stated above in the preface, "symbolic

resurrection"), and Jesus coming again to establish His kingdom on earth. This compromise with other postmodern thoughts against the knowledge of God should be cast down because God says in Jeremiah 23:36, "And the oracle of the LORD you shall mention no more. For every man's word will be his oracle, for you have perverted the words of the living God, the LORD of hosts, our God."

10. Messianic Jews[xxv] - called as Messianic Believers based upon "Messianic Judaism" movement. They are not necessarily Jews. They are different from Christianity and Judaism, deriving from them into their own faith in favor of Hebrew culture rather than western Greek culture. They committed to "Yeshua the Messiah" - not called as "Jesus Christ" English word because of its origin of western Greek culture - often misleading the public to think they are "Jews for Christ," who are the Christians stated in the Bible as we are, regardless of race or nationality. They emphasize the old covenantal duty of Jewish life from Torah - not called as the 5 books of Moses or Pentateuch because of the origin of the Greek word- with Hebrew tradition and culture applied in the overlook of the New Testament, called as "contextual approach."

So, Torah itself is accepted because Torah is the Pentateuch in the Bible. The contextual approach of the entire Bible itself is accepted to seek for God's will faithfully, but the contextual approach of Hebrew tradition and culture outside the Bible with some part of the New Testament is compromise and so not acceptable. I saw and tasted in the contextual approach combined between Korean traditional Shamanism after Korean War and the Bible. As God says in Matthew 5:8 "Blessed *are* the pure in heart, For they shall see God," with such compromise or impurity we could not see God or His will clearly.

11. Catholicism[xxvi] - developed in about 500 A.D. from Rome. "Catholic" means "universal." Catholics believe not only the Bible, not whole. For example, the 10 Commandments in Exodus 20:1-17 is deleted the 2nd one and divided the 10th one into two. The 2nd one is 20:4, "You shall not make for yourself a carved image—any likeness *of anything* that *is* in heaven above, or that *is* in the earth beneath, or that *is* in the water under the earth," while the 10th one is 20:17 "You shall not covet your neighbor's house;(here divided into two) you shall not covet your neighbor's wife, nor his male servant, nor his female servant, nor his ox, nor his donkey, nor anything that *is* your neighbor's." But also they believe or accept the Roman Catholic traditions (e.g., Peter as the first Pope, meaning "father"), Purgatory, God the mother (e.g., Virgin Mary), apocrypha, bowed image, salvation with faith plus work, geographical culture (e.g. ancestor worship of Confucianism stated above in the preface), etc. But very potential people are to be evangelized on only the Bible part. I see many converted brothers and sisters who are faithfully serving the Lord and His sheep.

12. Evolutionism[xxvii] – all things are a product of random chance and excessive time while the Bible says in Genesis 1 and 2 that God

as an intelligent Designer created all creatures (e.g., 1st day light, 2nd day heaven [firmament], 3rd day land, 4th day sun, moon, and star, 5th day birds and fish, 6th day animals, man and vegetables, and 7th day rest). Evolutionists allege that universe exploded from nothing, developing "big bang theory" of our current universe developed through sudden explosion from the "singularity (infinite small thing existed around 13.7 billion years ago)" just before nothing, contrary to the 1st law of thermodynamics (conservation law of energy) where energy can be changed from one state to another state (e.g. liquid to solid, and to gas, interchangeably) but it cannot be created or destroyed. Total amount of energy remains constant.

Also evolutionists insist that complexity has developed from simplicity over time against the 2nd law of Thermodynamics or the law of entropy (unusable energy) where in all energy exchanges in a closed system the usable energy of the state will decrease and entropy increase over time. Diversity of species evolved over time by natural selection according to "On the Origin of Species" of Charles Darwin, leading to transmutation of species and adaptive evolution not by proof of scientific mechanism but by sight observation. Transmutation of species (e.g. monkey to man; a banana to a spider, etc.) is contrary to gene modernly discovered in a biological organism. The hereditary unit located in chromosome of a cell in a biological organism is called as a gene composed of DNA containing nucleotide which consists of sugar (Deoxyribose), base (four kinds – adenine, guanine, cytosine, and thymine) and phosphate.

The sequence of nucleotides determines individual hereditary characteristics, proving intelligent design. Today we can find with DNA test our ancestors. Some Christians allow evolution as a tool of God's creation, known as "evolutional creation," which I had believed, in the above preface, until Chuck taught Genesis at church when I repented for purity. This compromise[xxviii] with the evolutionism as "a basic principle of the world" is a great danger to replace sovereign God's creation in Genesis, the core of the Christian faith.

13. New Age movement [New Age Spirituality][xxix] called as Cosmic Humanism, rejecting any religious doctrine but draw inspiration from Christianity, Buddhism, Hinduism, Islam, Judaism, Chinese folk religion (e.g. ancestor worship) with other philosophies such as Gnosticism, Spiritualism, Universalism, Confucianism, Taoism, Shinto, etc. in order to seek so called "universal truth" of the people who live in a postmodern culture, often using the term, "all is one" and "mind-body-spirit." The movement to seek "Universal Truth" with philosophies and religions is not according to Christ, so that it should be cast down even if "spirituality," "all is one," or "mind-body-spirit" term is often used, different meaning from in the Bible.

14. Atheism [xxx] - is the thought of the absence of god, by either rejection of god or god no existence, originated from skepticism or criticism of god and tended to philosophical thoughts of humanism, rationalism, or naturalism (virtues of natural world). But there is no one single thought because the person who has

the Atheism called as an "Atheist" or "non-believer" is seeking for whatever is a virtue as he by himself thinks, that is a self-led life." There is no the Bible basis, which should be cast down.

I have known a man who is generous and nice to people and introduces by himself as an atheist, doubting of deity but seeking a virtue which was discovered later. It was the virtue come from a novel about historical warfare in a country, human wisdom to deal people.   It is a sort of a religion because he as a finite man is seeking an infinite virtue. It is a self-imposed religion as God says in Colossians 2:23, "These things indeed have an appearance of wisdom in self-imposed religion......" When his family were introduced Gospel, all family members except him were converted to Christ. I personally ask you to pray for him because I love (AGAPE) him.

The standard of whether or not our thoughts are cast down is only the Bible, which is the Word of God. Contents of the Bible by themselves - without compromise with anything else - determine us simply to accept or not – not to conclude any judgmental words - as our only Lord Jesus Christ says in Matthew 5:8, "Blessed *are* the pure in heart, For they shall see God," because our supreme desire is to know Christ and be conformed in His image by the power of the Spirit.   For preaching, from the cast down thoughts we may develop parables close to hearers' thoughts without offense in the Spirit.

1.Self Questions to Confront:

(1) Can I put God in a man made frame?

(2) What is "Christian's devil possession?"

(3) What is difference between "the Word of Faith" and "the Venture in Faith"?

(4) What is Prosperity Gospel?

(5) What is Positive Thought doctrine?

(6) What is Feeling Good doctrine?

(7) What is Signs and Wonders Movement?

(8) What is Emerging Church?

(9) What is Evolutional Creation?

(10) What is New Age?

(11) What is Witness Lee?

(12) What is Messianic Jews?

(13) What's Seventh-day Adventists?

(14) What do Catholics believe?

(15) What is an atheist?

(16) Can I see my neighbor who doesn't believe in Christ? What is his thought?   Can I get a parable or an opening statement to deliver Gospel from these thoughts?

2.Verses to Meditate:

(1) 2 Corinthians 6:14-16,"Do not be unequally yoked together with unbelievers. For what fellowship has righteousness with lawlessness? And what communion has light with darkness? [15] And what accord has Christ with Belial? Or what part has a believer with an unbeliever? [16] And what agreement has the temple of God with idols? For you are the temple of the living God. As God has said"

(2) Romans 8:14, "For as many as are led by the Spirit of God, these are sons of God."

(3) 3 John 1:2. "Beloved, I pray that you may prosper in all things and be in health, just as your soul prospers."

(4) 1 Corinthians 12:9-10, "to another faith by the same Spirit, to another gifts of healings by the same Spirit, [10] to another the working of miracles, to another prophecy, to another discerning of spirits, to another *different* kinds of tongues, to another the interpretation of tongues."

(5) Jeremiah 23:36, "And the oracle of the LORD you shall mention no more. For every man's word will be his oracle, for you have perverted the words of the living God, the LORD of hosts, our God."

(6) Matthew 5:8,"Blessed *are* the pure in heart, For they shall see God."

(7) Matthew 20:28, "just as the Son of Man did not come to be served, but to serve, and to give His life a ransom for many."

B. Why Only The Bible?

God talked through Isaiah the prophet with Israelites about their sin, "Come now, and let us reason together," Says the LORD, " Though your sins are like scarlet, They shall be as white as snow; Though they are red like crimson, They shall be as wool. " Likewise, we are reasoning together why only the Bible. Only the Bible means the Bible excluding any books. Infinite God is absolute true. His truth doesn't dependent upon a person's defense or proof. Human truth is relative, being updated, added, deleted, or altered by a subsequent discovered truth. God neither errs nor fails while a person usually errs or fails, because God is sufficient as Jesus says, "it is finished," on cross. God is absolutely true. So, His word or the Word of God is absolute true. If the Bible is the Word of God, the Bible also is absolute true.

We as finite people can't prove the absolute truth of the Bible but with finite reasons can prove some truth of the Bible. So the Bible can be proved to be true from science, archaeology, prophecy, and personal experience. [xxxi] We can't understand "absolute truth" of the Bible unless the Holy Spirit given by infinite God reveals His reason to us, called as "revelation." Then, the Spirit makes us understand the Bible as God says in 2 Timothy 3:16, "All Scripture *is* given by inspiration of God, and *is* profitable for doctrine, for reproof, for correction, for instruction in righteousness." Inspiration means that "God the Holy Spirit in a unique supernatural way so that written words of the Scripture writers controlled by God were also the words of God."[xxxii] Here "inspiration" the English

Word is "THEOPHNEUSTOS" the Greek Word in the original Bible, a special meaning of "God-breathed," like "Love" the English word previously described in the Greek Word in 4 types special meanings whose AGAPE is divine unconditional love. "All Scripture is inspired by God" means especially "All Scripture is breathed by God" through writers, concluding "the Word of God."

1. The Bible can be proved to be true with following four (4) human reasons. [xxxiii xxxiv]

a. A reason from science.

(1) The scientific discovery of the "circle of the earth" proved Isaiah 40:22a, "*It is* He who sits above the circle of the earth ......" to be true in the Bible. (2) Psalm 135:7, "He causes the vapors to ascend from the ends of the earth; He makes lightning for the rain; He brings the wind out of His treasuries, " Job 36:27, "For He draws up drops of water, Which distill as rain from the mist," and Isaiah 55:10a, "For as the rain comes down, and the snow from heaven, And do not return there, But water the earth, And make it bring forth and bud ......," in the Bible were proved to be true by Scientists' discovery of the hydrological cycle of weather. (3)Geologists' discovery that earth orbits by slope in the space to keep equally balanced weights proved Isaiah 40:12, "Who has measured the waters in the hollow of His hand, Measured heaven with a span And calculated the dust of the earth in a measure? Weighed the mountains in scales And the hills in a balance?" in the Bible to be true.

With the reason from science, the Bible is proved to be true.

b. *A reason from Archaeology*

The Bible can be proved to be true from a reason from archaeology. Archaeologist Nelson Glueck's discovery of "the remains of a big refining factory, for copper and iron, which was traded for gold to Solomon, and silver and ivory" is conformed with 1 King 9:28, "And they went to Ophir, and acquired four hundred and twenty talents of gold from there, and brought *it* to King Solomon," and 1 Kings 10:22, "For the king had merchant ships at sea with the fleet of Hiram. Once every three years the merchant ships came bringing gold, silver, ivory, apes, and monkeys" Archaeologists' discovery of "Dinosaurs" proved "Behemoth" in Job 40:15, " Look now at the behemoth, which I made *along* with you; He eats grass like an ox," as named modernly Dinosaurs, to be true in the Bible. More archeological proofs can be seen in the "Halley's Bible Handbook."

With the reason from archaeology, the Bible is proved to be true in history.

c. *A reason from fulfilled the Bible prophecy.*

Isaiah's prophecy (discussed below, the 1st meaning of "foretelling") between 745 through 695 BC in Isaiah 7:14, "Therefore the Lord Himself will give you a sign: Behold, the virgin shall conceive and bear a Son, and shall call His name Immanuel," was about 700 years later fulfilled the birth of Jesus.   Daniel's prophetic interpretation of Nebuchadnezzar the Babylonian King during 606 BC through 536 BC in Daniel 2:38-40, "and wherever the children of men dwell, or the beasts of the field and the birds of the heaven, He has given *them* into your hand, and has made you ruler over them all—you *are* this head of gold. [39] But after you shall arise another kingdom inferior to yours (2:32 "silver"); then another, a third kingdom of bronze, which shall rule over all the earth. [40] And the fourth kingdom shall be as strong as iron, inasmuch as iron breaks in pieces and shatters everything; and like iron that crushes, *that kingdom* will break in pieces and crush all the others," was fulfilled historically when Babylon (gold) was conquered by Persia (silver) in 536 BC, Persia conquered by Greece (bronze) in 331 BC, and Greece conquered by Rome (iron) in 63 BC to prove the Bible is true. Peter W. Stoner, a scientist and mathematician, calculated mathematical probability or chance to fulfill Ezekiel's prophecy about Tyre's destruction in the consequence of 7 events in Ezekiel 26:3-6, "Therefore thus says the Lord GOD: 'Behold, I *am* against you, O Tyre, and will cause many nations to come up against you, as the sea causes its waves to come up....'" The probability of all 7 events occurring as Ezekiel prophesied was one in 400 million, but all seven events occurred historically. They calculated the probability of the fall of Babylon in Isaiah 13:19," And Babylon, the glory of kingdoms, The beauty of the Chaldeans' pride, Will be as when God overthrew Sodom and Gomorrah," at one in 100 billion, yet everything was fulfilled historically. Other hundreds of Biblical prophecy were fulfilled far beyond mathematical probability calculation, human expectation, wisdom, or reasons.

With this reason from fulfilled the Bible prophecy, the Bible is proved to be true.

d. A reason to change lives from the Bible.

In the preface, I as a Buddhist did not understand self studying the Bible. But the deacon taught the Bible that converted me from a Buddhist to a Christian life. The Bible, taught by me, converted sisters from Catholics, converted a sister from a Jehovah's Witness, a sister from "the Church of Christ, Scientist," a brother from a Mormon, a brother from a prisoner, etc. Also, the Bible made converters grow spiritually. We could listen to thousands of people's testimonies about how the Bible has changed their lives on radio, TV, or Internet.

With the reason to change lives from the Bible is the Bible proved to be true.

Therefore, the Bible is proved to be true with the above 4 reasons.

However, this proof is not sufficient for the Bible's "absolute truth." The Bible in John 17:3, "And this is eternal life, that they may know You, the only true God, and Jesus Christ whom You have sent," declares "only true God" which is absolute true. In John 17:17, "Sanctify them by Your truth. Your word is truth," God's word is truth. In John 1:1 "In the beginning was the Word, and the Word was with God, and the Word was God," the Word (written word LOGOS) was God. Unlike human relative truth, updated, added, deleted, or altered by a discovered truth, the Bible declares the prohibition of its alteration in Deuteronomy 4:2, "You shall not add to the word which I command you, nor take from it, that you may keep the commandments of the LORD your God which I command you." In Psalm 19:7, "The law of the LORD *is* perfect, converting the soul; The testimony of the LORD *is* sure, making wise the simple," the Bible is perfect, that is, infallible, inerrant, or authoritative. In John 14:6, "Jesus said to him, "I am the way, the truth, and the life. No one comes to the Father except through Me," Jesus is the truth and no one comes to the Father except through the truth. So, Jesus is only the truth or absolute truth. In John 5:39, "You search the Scriptures, for in them you think you have eternal life; and these are they which testify of Me," the Scriptures or the Bible testify of Jesus the truth. Those verses in the Bible declare that the Bible is the absolute truth, unlike relative truth allowing subsequent alteration. In Matthew 28:18, "And Jesus came and spoke to them, saying, "All authority has been given to Me in heaven and on earth," all authority has given to Jesus the truth. So, the Bible declares that the Bible is absolutely authoritative.

We live on a negligible earth planet in the system of Sun which is one of the stars in one Milky Way galaxy of more than 170 billion galaxies[xxxv] in the universe created by God, proving truth of the Bible (the Word of God) like the discovery of a grain of sands of all beaches in the earth. It will be still proved continually toward the absolute truth of the Bible until the first heaven and earth are passed away.

Therefore, all human reasons to prove that the Bible is true are not sufficient to prove the Bible is absolutely true or absolutely authoritative. We can't understand "absolute truth" of the Bible unless the Holy Spirit given by infinite God reveals His wisdom to us.

1.Self Questions to Confront:
(1) Is God's truth dependent upon my wisdom or defense?
(2) What do "revelation" and "inspiration" mean?

(3) Which ways can I prove the Bible is true?

(4) Are human proofs sufficient to prove "Absolute truth" of the Bible? How can I understand the Absolute Truth?

2.Verses to Meditate:

(1) 2 Timothy 3:16 "All Scripture *is* given by inspiration of God, and *is* profitable for doctrine, for reproof, for correction, for instruction in righteousness,"

(2) Job 36:27 "For He draws up drops of water, Which distill as rain from the mist,"

(3) Job 40:15 "Look now at the behemoth, which I made *along* with you; He eats grass like an ox."

(4) Isaiah 7:14 "Therefore the Lord Himself will give you a sign: Behold, the virgin shall conceive and bear a Son, and shall call His name Immanuel."

(5) Psalm 19:7 "The law of the LORD *is* perfect, converting the soul; The testimony of the LORD *is* sure, making wise the simple"

2. Why not others than the Bible?

a. Answer

The Teachings of the Buddha (Dharma), Hindu's Writing, Vedas, Confucius' Teachings, Qur'an, Talmud, Apocrypha, Science and Health with Key to the Scriptures, The Book of Mormon, and New World Translation of the Holy Scriptures are not all the Word of God because each of them was in part or all written by men, although some part of it may be the Word of God.   For preaching, from the following books other than the Bible we may develop parables or open statements close to hearers' thoughts with the Agape love of Jesus. Some books I experienced were discussed in the preface above.

b. Proof with reasons

The following books are proved not to be all the Word of God as follows:

（1） Teachings of Buddha (Dharma)[xxxvi]-   Dharma include the teaching of Buddha, the founder of Buddhism, about eliminating self desire causing suffering to reach Par-nirvana (nonexistent self state), merciful charity practice, wisdom, rebirth to an animal or man, depending upon well self disciplined behavior during his social and individual life in regulated classes.   The teachings about philosophy, traditions, and religious practice are all about human words, not the Word of God. I testified in some part in the above preface.

（2） Hindu's writing[xxxvii]   – The writing is divided into "Revealed" (Sruti) and "Remembers" (Smrti) writing about the dominant cultic religion of India. It emphasizes (1) dharma (righteous duty), with its resulting ritual and social observance, and often both (2) mystical contemplation to realize his identity with God, reaching the freedom from the cycle of life, and (3) ascetic practices. The Hindu's writing is not the Word of God because the writing was written by a man.

(3) Vedas (wisdom knowledge) [xxxviii]– Four parts of hymns (Samhita), rituals (Brahmana), theology(Aranyaka), and philosophy (Upanishads) that comprise the earliest Hindu sacred writing was basically written about human wisdom knowledge by a man. So, Vedas is not the Word of God.

(4) Confucius' Teachings[xxxix] - He as a Chinese philosopher was the founder of Confucianism which is a philosophical and religious system. He set up the 5 basic relationships between (1) Ruler and Ruled, (2) Father and Son, (3) Husband and Wife, (4) Elder and Younger, and (5) Friend and Friend for the duty of loyalties. Where the first four ones are in hierarchy, the higher (ruler, father, husband, and elder) should give mercy to the lower (ruled, son, wife, and younger) and the lower must obey the higher (which gave a birth of a coercive ruler). In the last one, friendly relationship is required. The duties extend to the decedent, "ancestor worship." By disciplining by themselves with the duties, they believe that they could be perfect. So, Confucius' Teachings as a man's teaching is not the Word of God.

(5) Qur'an[Koran][xl] – The book, accepted by Muslims as revelations made to Muhammad by Allah through the angle Gabriel, was written by Allah, not trinity God but one God. To get eternal life in heaven, a man must do service, submission, and obedience to God, who has no intimate personal relationship with him but judges sinners, unbelievers, or the proud. The book was written by Allah the different God from the Trinity God who loves

the world including sinners and who wants to have intimate relationship with us. So, Koran is not the Word of God.

> I met some Muslims who know Jesus, Moses, David or other Characters in the Bible, stated in the Koran, from which we might bring parables close to their situation for preaching led by the Spirit or the Spirit led preaching.

(6) Talmud[xli] – The book written about Jewish tradition by ancient Rabbis contains two sections of the Mishnah and the Gemara founded Orthodox Judaism. Talmud is not the Word of God because it was written about human tradition by men. Before called a pastor, I worked with my partner, a Jews, who practiced in Talmud as to "how to fish" rather than "fish itself." It's so harsh when his children born in the States did not want to learn the Hebrew and then under his severe threat they got taught it.

(7) Apocrypha[xlii] – Septuagint and Vulgate in Apocrypha are not the Word of God because those were excluded from the cannons of Old Testament which is included in the Bible. The apocrypha is called often for the 14 books written by uncertain authors between the Old Testament and the New Testament, during 1st through 3rd Centuries BC. They were neither used by the Jews as a part of the Hebrews Scriptures nor used by Jesus. Therefore they are excluded from the Bible divinely inspired. They are not the Word of God.

(8) Science and Health with Key to the Scriptures[xliii] – The book written by Mary Baker Eddy founding "the Church of Christ, Scientist" in 1879 derived from the Bible but emphasizing healing through prayers in the Bible over modern medical treatment and added cause and effect science theory in the book and rejected the reality of sin, sickness, death, and the material world in the Bible. This Book is not all the Word of God because the book was in part excluded from the Bible and in part added by the man. The Christian Science Monitor daily newspaper has been published.

(9) The Book of Mormon – published with use of Mormon the prophet not in the Bible in 1830 by Joseph Smith, Jr. Mormons practice the book of Mormon in the name of (1) the Church of Jesus Christ of Latter-day Saints (LDS church), (2) Mormon fundamentalists who are still practicing polygamy, or (3) Community of Christ.

Deriving from the book, Adam-God Doctrine, "Adam is our Father and our God," cited on April 9, 1952 Journal of Discourse, Vol 1 Pages 50-51 by Brigham Young [xliv]is contrary to the Bible, "God the creator made Adam the creature," in Genesis 2:7, "LORD God formed man of the dust of the ground, and breathed into his nostrils the breath of life; and man became a living being."

"Adam is the Father of Jesus Christ" cited on Women of Mormon, p 179 is contrary to God the Father is the Father of Jesus Christ in Matthew 3:17 "And suddenly a voice *came* from heaven, saying, "This is My beloved Son, in whom I am well pleased."

"Jesus was born of a virgin but not conceived by the Holy Spirit" on April 9, 1852 Brigham Young's sermon is contrary to Matthew 1:20 "… is conceived in her is of the Holy Spirit."

Polygamy, marriage between one man and more than one woman, is contrary to marriage between one man and one woman, in Matthew 19:5, "…… *a man shall leave his father and mother and be joined to his wife, and the two shall become one flesh'*?"

Marriage life resurrected after physical death is contrary to Matthew 22:30, "For in the resurrection they neither marry nor are given in marriage, but are like angels of God in heaven."

"Salvation comes by faith with human works" is contrary to salvation comes only by faith in Ephesians 2:8-9," For by grace you have been saved through faith, and that not of yourselves; *it is* the gift of God, [9] not of works, lest anyone should boast," and Isaiah 64:6, "we are all like an unclean *thing,* And all our righteousnesses *are* like filthy rags; We all fade as a leaf, And our iniquities, like the wind, Have taken us away." The historical background of the Book of Mormon is never archeologically proved in America.

(10) New World Translation of the Holy Scriptures [Watch Tower] – translated by the Watch Tower Society of Jehovah's Witnesses,

founded by Charles Russell and Judge Rutherford, is different from the Bible. "The Word was a god" in the Translation is different from "The Word was God" in John 1:1 of the Bible.

The "Study of Scriptures" written by Russell and Rutherford denying the divinity of Christ and alleging Jesus Christ is a spirit and archangel Michael before being born[xlv] is contrary to Jesus' incarnation (God becomes flesh) in John 1:14 "And the Word became flesh and dwelt among us," and in Matthew 1:23, ""*Behold, the virgin shall be with child, and bear a Son, and they shall call His name Immanuel,*" which is translated, "God with us."

Their belief of "eternal life on earth" is contrary to "a new heaven and a new earth" of Revelation 21:1," Now I saw a new heaven and a new earth, for the first heaven and the first earth had passed away. Also there was no more sea."

Their belief of "(1) when Jesus came to earth from heaven, He laid aside angelic (or spiritual) nature and lived as a man and (2) when He left earth, He laid aside his human nature" is contrary to the incarnation, that is, God's being made manifest in a human body in John 1:14 (above), and Jesus' resurrection with glorified body in John 20:27, "Then He said to Thomas, "Reach your finger here, and look at My hands; and reach your hand *here,* and put *it* into My side. Do not be unbelieving, but believing," and John 21:12 "Jesus said to them, "Come *and* eat breakfast." Yet none of the disciples dared ask Him, "Who are You?"—knowing that it was the Lord."

Their belief that "144,000 are Jehovah's Witnesses," is contrary to the Children of Israel in Revelation 7:4, "And I heard the number of those who were sealed. One hundred *and* forty-four thousand of all the tribes of the children of Israel *were* sealed."

Their interpretation of Leviticus 3:17 "*This shall be* a perpetual statute throughout your generations in all your dwellings: you shall eat neither fat nor blood," as refusal of blood transfusions is wrong because eating is not transfusion. Further, 1 Corinthians 8:8 "But food does not commend us to God; for neither if we eat are we the better, nor if we do not eat are we the worse," and Galatians 5:4, "You have become estranged from Christ, you who *attempt to* be justified by law; you have fallen from grace," discourages their refusal of blood transfusions as well as of military service.

To allure a Christian into them, they often attack the Christmas day or Jesus' birthday, December 25, 0 AD.   In the church history, in 315 AD Constantine the Roman Emperor declared Christianity as the Roman Religion. He adopted the Babylonian Pagan Celebration of "Saturnalia," congratulating the birth of "Tammuz" whom virgin Simiramus bore.   The birthday of Tammuz the Babylonian pagan god was replaced with the Christmas day.

Also, the Virgin Simiramus goddess delivered the birth of Ashtart goddess. Tammuz god married Ashtart goddess, but Tammuz was killed by a hog while he was hunting. Ashtart wept with pain until spring, when dead Tammuz resurrected from his grave. That's called as Easter, in English sound.

Archeologically, today Jesus' birth day might have been born in October in 4 BC. But it is indisputable historical fact of Jesus who was born on the earth by Virgin Mary and was resurrected bodily. Although today Christmas day or Easter day is contaminated with commercialism, no Christians who celebrate Jesus' birth on the Christmas day or Jesus' resurrection on the Easter day celebrate the Babylonian pagan god Tammuz or goddess Ashtart. So, their false doctrines have no room to replace the Word of God but God loves them in purity with His broken heart, waiting for their coming back to Him soon in 2 Peter 3:9, "The Lord is not slack concerning *His* promise, as some count slackness, but is longsuffering toward us, not willing that any should perish but that all should come to repentance."

Therefore, the above books other than the Bible are not all the Word of God because each of them was in part or all written by men, although some part of it may be the Word of God. Exclusions other than the Bible are proved.

For the Spirit led preaching, we may derive parables for hearers from the above books.

Now, "only" the Bible is proved to be true with the above reasons. However, all human reasons to prove that only the Bible is true are not sufficient to prove the Bible is absolutely true and absolutely authoritative. We can't understand "absolute truth" of the Bible unless the Holy Spirit given by infinite God reveals His wisdom to us, finite men. In 1 Corinthians 2:14, "But the natural man does not receive the things of the Spirit of God, for they are foolishness to him; nor can he know *them,* because they are spiritually discerned," the Holy Spirit is the only one who can prove that the Bible is absolutely true and absolutely authoritative as God is, resulting in the Word of God, and He reveals this absolute truth of the Bible in the heart and mind of Christian, known as spiritually minded Christian, whom He indwells, being led, being filled, and being overflowed. In 1 Corinthians 2:1-5, "And I, brethren, when I came to you, did not come with excellence of speech or of wisdom declaring to you the testimony of God. [2] For I determined not to know anything among you except Jesus Christ and Him crucified. [3] I was with you in weakness, in fear, and in much trembling. [4] And my speech and my preaching *were* not with persuasive words of human wisdom, but in demonstration of the Spirit and of power, [5] that your faith should not be in the wisdom of men but in the power of God," Paul taught that preaching the testimony of God is simple gospel in demonstration of the Spirit and of the divine power, neither with persuasive words of human wisdom nor with excellence of speech. Although the gospel appears foolish to the natural men or the unbelievers, the simple gospel is the power of God to the believers in 1 Corinthians 1:18 "For the message of the cross is foolishness to those who are perishing, but to us who are being saved it is the power of God." Therefore, the Holy Spirit should work in the heart of the man. Then, he can understand the absolute truth of the Word of God because of the Spirit, without human proof but upon faith in John 20:29, "Jesus said to him, "Thomas, because you have seen Me, you have believed. Blessed *are* those who have not seen and *yet* have believed." "

As Jesus says in John 14:26, "But the Helper, the Holy Spirit, whom the Father will send in My name, He will teach you all things, and bring to your remembrance all things that I said to you," the Holy Spirit will teach him all things.

In 2 Timothy 3:16 "All Scripture *is* given by inspiration of God, and *is* profitable for doctrine, for reproof, for correction, for instruction in righteousness," all scripture which means the 66 books of the Bible is inspired by God.

God prohibits either to add or to delete any part of the Bible to anyone in Matthew 5:18-19, "For assuredly, I say to you, till heaven and earth pass away, one jot or one tittle will by no means pass from the law till all is fulfilled. [19] Whoever therefore breaks one of the least of these commandments, and teaches men so, shall be called least in the kingdom of heaven; but whoever does and teaches *them,* he shall be called great in the kingdom of heaven," and in Revelation 22:18-19, "For I testify to everyone who hears the words of the prophecy (including forth-telling with foretelling, discussed below) of this book: If anyone adds to these things, God will add to him the plagues that are written in this book; [19] and if anyone takes away from the words of the book of this prophecy, God shall take away his part from the Book of Life, from the holy city, and *from* the things which are written in this book."

Other gospels than the Bible are not allowed as Paul says in Galatians 1:7-9, "which is not another; but there are some who trouble you and want to pervert the gospel of Christ. [8] But even if we, or an angel from heaven, preach any other gospel to you than what we have preached to you, let him be accursed. [9] As we have said before, so now I say again, if anyone preaches any other gospel to you than what you have received, let him be accursed." It is spiritually discerned that above other books than the Bible are not all the Word of God and that only the Bible is the Word of God.

1.Self Questions to Confront:

(1) What is Dharma? I a Buddhist around me? Can I deliver Gospel through prayer?

(2) What is Smrti? What is Vedas? Is a Hindu around me? Can I deliver Gospel through prayer?

(3) What is Confucianism?

(4) What is Koran? Is a Muslim around me? Can I deliver Gospel through prayer?

(5) What is Talmud? Is a Jews around me? Can I deliver Gospel through prayer?

(6) What is Apocrypha?

(7) What is "Science and Health with Key to the Scripture"? Can I deliver Gospel to the Church of Christ Scientist through prayer?

(8) What is the Book of Mormon? Can I deliver Gospel to a Mormon through prayer?

(9) What is New World Translation of the Holy Scriptures? Can I deliver Gospel to a Jehovah's witness through prayer?

2.Verses to Meditate:

(1) John 17:3 "And this is eternal life, that they may know You, the only true God, and Jesus Christ whom You have sent."

(2) John 17:17 "Sanctify them by Your truth. Your word is truth."

(3) 2 Peter 3:9 "The Lord is not slack concerning *His* promise, as some count slackness, but is longsuffering toward us, not willing that any should perish but that all should come to repentance."

(4) Galatians 1:7-9 "which is not another; but there are some who trouble you and want to pervert the gospel of Christ. [8] But even if we, or an angel from heaven, preach any other gospel to you than what we have preached to you, let him be accursed. [9] As we have said before, so now I say again, if anyone preaches any other gospel to you than what you have received, let him be accursed."

1. Faith Statement

First, pray for the Lord's revelation into your heart, and then meditate the faithful God's word leading your faith in the Spirit.

1. We Believe: the Bible to be the inspired, the only infallible, authoritative Word of God and inerrant in the original writings; in 2 Timothy 3:16-17, "All Scripture *is* given by inspiration of God, and *is* profitable for doctrine, for reproof, for correction, for instruction in righteousness, [17] that the man of God may be complete, thoroughly equipped for every good work," in Deuteronomy 4:2, "You shall not add to the word which I command you, nor take from it, that you may keep the commandments of the LORD your God which I command you" and in Revelation 22:18-19, "For I testify to everyone who hears the words of the prophecy of this book: If anyone adds to these things, God will add to him the plagues that are written in this book; [19] and if anyone takes away from the words of the book of this prophecy, God shall take away his part from the Book of Life, from the holy city, and *from* the things which are written in this book."

2. We Believe: there is one God, eternally and equally existent in three persons, Father, Son, and Holy Spirit; in Matthew 3:16-17,"When He had been baptized, Jesus came up immediately from the water; and behold, the heavens were opened to Him,

and He saw the Spirit of God descending like a dove and alighting upon Him. [17] And suddenly a voice *came* from heaven, saying, "This is My beloved Son, in whom I am well pleased," in Genesis 1:1, "In the beginning God (Elohim, three plural) created the heavens and the earth," and in Genesis 1:26, "Then God said, "Let Us (plural, not Me) make man in Our image, according to Our likeness...."

3. We Believe: (1) in the deity of our Lord Jesus Christ in John 1:34, "And I have seen and testified that this is the Son of God," and in John 1:49, "Nathanael answered and said to Him, "Rabbi, You are the Son of God! You are the King of Israel!; (2) in His virgin birth in Matthew 1:23, "*"Behold, the virgin shall be with child, and bear a Son, and they shall call His name Immanuel,"* which is translated, "God with us"; (3) in His sinless life in Hebrews 4:15, "For we do not have a High Priest who cannot sympathize with our weaknesses, but was in all *points* tempted as *we are, yet* without sin,"(4) in His literal miracles in John 2:1-11(Water turning to Wine), John 4:46-54 (a nobleman son at the point of death healed), John 5:1-18 (infirmity man healed), John 6:6-13 (five loves two fish for 5000 men), and so on; (5) in His vicarious and atoning death through His shed blood in 1 Corinthians 15:3, "For I delivered to you first of all that which I also received: that Christ died for our sins according to the Scriptures';" (6) in His bodily resurrection in 1 Corinthians 15:4, "and that He was buried, and that He rose again the third day according to the

Scriptures;" (7) in His ascension to the right hand of the Father, in Acts 1:9, "Now when He had spoken these things, while they watched, He was taken up, and a cloud received Him out of their sight"; and (8) in His personal return in power and glory in Acts 1:11, "who also said, "Men of Galilee, why do you stand gazing up into heaven? This *same* Jesus, who was taken up from you into heaven, will so come in like manner as you saw Him go into heaven."

4. We Believe: in the terms of The Apostles' Creed,

"I believe in God the Father Almighty, Maker of heaven and earth, and in Jesus Christ, His only Son, our Lord: Who was conceived by the Holy Spirit, born of the Virgin Mary,

Suffered under Pontius Pilate (in John 19:1, "So then Pilate took Jesus and scourged *Him*") was crucified, dead, and buried. He descended into hell (in 1 Peter 3:19 "by whom also He went and preached to the spirits in prison").

The third day He arose again from the dead. He ascended into heaven and sits on the right hand of God the Father Almighty, from thence He shall come to judge the quick and the dead.

I believe in the Holy Spirit, the Holy Universal Church, the communion of saints, the forgiveness of sins, the resurrection of the body, and the life everlasting. Amen,"

Which are within the zone of the authoritative Word of God, as expressing fundamental facts of Christian Faith (Jesus' disciples declared "The Apostles" Creed" as their faith against a heresy or a cult, in church history. For the same purpose, we may use this creed.).

5. We Believe: in (1) the lost and sinful person must be saved only through faith in Ephesians 2:8-9 "For by grace you have been saved through faith, and that not of yourselves; *it is* the gift of God, [9] not of works, lest anyone should boast," and in (2) person's only hope of redemption is through the shed blood of Jesus Christ, the Son of God, in Hebrews 9:22, "And according to the law almost all things are purified with blood, and without shedding of blood there is no remission."

6. We Believe: in the present ministry of the Holy Spirit by whose (1) indwelling in 1 Corinthians 6:19"Or do you not know that your body is the temple of the Holy Spirit *who is* in you, whom you have from God, and you are not your own?" and (2) leading in Romans 8:14, "For as many as are led by the Spirit of God, these are sons of God," the Christian is enabled to live a Godly life.

7. We Believe: two ordinances of both Baptism and the Lord's Supper given to the Church by Christ, through (1) water baptism

by immersion in Matthew 3:16,"When He had been baptized, Jesus came up immediately from the water..." and (2) communion in 1 Corinthians 11:24-25, "and when He had given thanks, He broke *it* and said, "Take, eat; this is My body which is broken for you; do this in remembrance of Me." [25] In the same manner *He* also *took* the cup after supper, saying, "This cup is the new covenant in My blood. This do, as often as you drink *it,* in remembrance of Me," open to all believers.

8. We Believe: in light of 1 Timothy 5:22," Do not lay hands on anyone hastily, nor share in other people's sins; keep yourself pure," the laying hands on persons as mere methodology of prayer (1) for acknowledgment of ordained pastors, elders, and deacons, (2) for healing, (3) for water baptism, (4) for the baptism of the Holy Spirit in John 1:33 "I did not know Him, but He who sent me to baptize with water said to me, 'Upon whom you see the Spirit descending, and remaining on Him, this is He who baptizes with the Holy Spirit.," or (5) for receiving gifts of the Spirit.

9. We Believe: in the Work of the Holy Spirit with (1) gifts in 1 Corinthians 12:1-11 (word of wisdom, word of knowledge, faith, healing, miracle, prophecy, discerning of spirits, tongues, interpretation of tongues, etc), (2) fruit in Galatians 5:22-23, "But the fruit of the Spirit is love, joy, peace, longsuffering, kindness,

goodness, faithfulness, [23] gentleness, self-control. Against such there is no law," (3) leading in Romans 8:14, "...led by the Spirit," and (4) teaching in 1 John 2:27, "But the anointing which you have received from Him abides in you, and you do not need that anyone teach you; but as the same anointing teaches you concerning all things, and is true, and is not a lie, and just as it has taught you, you will abide in Him."

10. We Believe: in Ephesians 1:22-23,"And He put all *things* under His feet, and gave Him *to be* head over all *things* to the church, which is His body, the fullness of Him who fills all in all," in (1) the spiritual unity of believers in our Lord Jesus Christ and in (2) "one church(*Eklesia*) on the earth," the living spiritual body, of which Christ is the Head and all regenerated persons are members.

11. We Believe: chronologically in (1) the rapture of the Church or the 1st part of the 1st resurrection (Luke 21:36,"Watch therefore, and pray always that you may be counted worthy to escape all these things that will come to pass, and to stand before the Son of Man," and 1 Thessalonians 4:16-18, "For the Lord Himself will descend from heaven with a shout, with the voice of an archangel, and with the trumpet of God. And the dead in Christ will rise first. [17] Then we who are alive *and* remain shall be caught up together with them in the clouds to meet the Lord in

the air. And thus we shall always be with the Lord. [18] Therefore comfort one another with these words"), (2) Great Tribulation (Daniel 9 and Revelation 6-18), (3) Jesus' 2nd coming on earth and (4) Judgment for beheaded Christians unto the 2nd part of the 1st resurrection of life (Revelation 20:4 "And I saw thrones, and they sat on them, and judgment was committed to them. Then *I saw* the souls of those who had been beheaded for their witness to Jesus and for the Word of God, who had not worshiped the beast or his image, and had not received *his* mark on their foreheads or on their hands. And they lived and reigned with Christ for a thousand years,"), (5) Millennium Kingdom (Revelation 20:5-6 "But the rest of the dead did not live again until the thousand years were finished. This *is* the first resurrection. [6] Blessed and holy *is* he who has part in the first resurrection. Over such the second death has no power, but they shall be priests of God and of Christ, and shall reign with Him a thousand years."), (6) great white throne judgment for 2nd resurrection of damnation (Revelation 20:11-15 "Then I saw a great white throne and Him who sat on it, from whose face the earth and the heaven fled away. And there was found no place for them. [12] And I saw the dead, small and great, standing before God, and books were opened. And another book was opened, which is *the Book* of Life. And the dead were judged according to their works, by the things which were written in the books. [13] The sea gave up the dead who were in it, and Death and Hades delivered up the dead who were in them. And they were judged, each one according to his works. [14] Then Death and Hades were cast into the lake of fire. This is the second death. [15] And anyone not found written in the Book of Life was cast into the lake of fire.") and (7) new heaven and earth (Revelation 21:1 "Now I saw a new heaven and a new earth, for the first heaven and the first earth had passed away. Also there was no more sea.")

So, the rapture of the Church will be in pre-tribulation, and in the pre-millennial return of Christ.

Therefore, we believe in all above statements in the Bible.

1.Self Questions to Confront:

  (1) What does Trinity mean?

  (2) What does Deity mean?

  (3) Did Jesus resurrect?

  (4) How can I save?

  (5) What's the present ministry of the Spirit?

  (6) What's difference between the gifts and the fruit of the Spirit?

  (7) Is my life fruitful for Jesus Christ? Am I fruitful for the Kingdom of God? Is the fruit

  of the Spirit coming forth from my life?

  (8) Am I in the spiritual unity of believers?

  (9) What do "pre-tribulation" and "pre-millennium" mean?

2.Verses to Meditate:

  (1) Matthew 3:16-17, "When He had been baptized, Jesus came up immediately from the water; and behold, the heavens were opened to Him, and He saw the Spirit of God descending like a dove and alighting upon Him. [17] And suddenly a voice *came* from heaven, saying, "This is

My beloved Son, in whom I am well pleased."

(2) John 1:49, "Nathanael answered and said to Him, "Rabbi, You are the Son of God! You are the King of Israel!"

(3) Ephesians 2:8-9, "For by grace you have been saved through faith, and that not of yourselves; *it is* the gift of God, [9] not of works, lest anyone should boast."

(4) 1 Corinthians 6:19" Or do you not know that your body is the temple of the Holy Spirit *who is* in you, whom you have from God, and you are not your own?"

(5) Roman 8:14,"For as many as are led by the Spirit of God, these are sons of God."

(6) 1 Corinthians 12:1-11,"Now concerning spiritual *gifts,* brethren, I do not want you to be ignorant: [2] You know that you were Gentiles, carried away to these dumb idols, however you were led. [3] Therefore I make known to you that no one speaking by the Spirit of God calls Jesus accursed, and no one can say that Jesus is Lord except by the Holy Spirit. [4] There are diversities of gifts, but the same Spirit. [5] There are differences of ministries, but the same Lord. [6] And there are diversities of activities, but it is the same God who works all in all. [7] But the manifestation of the Spirit is given to each one for the profit *of all:* [8] for to one is given the word of wisdom through the Spirit, to another the word of knowledge through the same Spirit, [9] to another faith by the same Spirit, to another gifts of healings by the same Spirit, [10] to another the working of miracles, to another prophecy, to another discerning of spirits, to another *different* kinds of tongues, to another the interpretation of tongues. [11] But one and the same Spirit works all these things, distributing to each one individually as He wills."

(7) Ephesians 1:22-23, "And He put all *things* under His feet, and gave

Him *to be* head over all *things* to the church, [23] which is His body, the fullness of Him who fills all in all."

(8) 1 Thessalonians 4:16-18, "For the Lord Himself will descend from heaven with a shout, with the voice of an archangel, and with the trumpet of God. And the dead in Christ will rise first. [17] Then we who are alive *and* remain shall be caught up together with them in the clouds to meet the Lord in the air. And thus we shall always be with the Lord. [18] Therefore comfort one another with these words."

2. Whole Counsel of God

Paul said before the Ephesians Elders in Acts 20:27, "For I have not shunned to declare to you the whole counsel of God." Also Jesus says in Matthew 4:4, "But He answered and said, "It is written, *'Man shall not live by bread alone, but by every word that proceeds from the mouth of God.'*" God warns us in Hebrews 5:12-14, "For though by this time you ought to be teachers, you need *someone* to teach you again the first principles of the oracles of God; and you have come to need milk and not solid food. [13] For everyone who partakes *only* of milk *is* unskilled in the word of righteousness, for he is a babe. [14] But solid food belongs to those who are of full age, *that is,* those who by reason of use have their senses exercised to discern both good and evil." So we need solid food from milk for full age, or spiritual maturity, to discern both good and evil.

To deliver the whole counsel of God or every word, verse by verse inductive study or teaching is most effective to us. But deductive topical study or teaching is designed to make us understand a topic or main theme, citing verses relevant to the topic.

The Bible, the Word of God, or The Whole Counsel of God contains 66 Books, whose the Old Testament is 39 Books and the New Testament is 27 Books.

For the Old Testament, here are 17 Historical Books, 5 Poetical Books, and 17 Prophetic Books.

The 17 Historical Books are Genesis, Exodus, Leviticus, Numbers, Deuteronomy – the first 5 books called as "Pentateuch or Five Books – Joshua, Judges, Ruth, I Samuel, II Samuel, I Kings, II Kings, I Chronicles, II Chronicles, Ezra, Nehemiah, and Esther.

The 5 Poetical Books are Job, Psalms, Proverbs, Ecclesiastes, and Song of Solomon.

The 17 Prophetic Books are Isaiah, Jeremiah, Lamentations, Ezekiel, Daniel – the first 5 books called as "Major Prophets and the last 12 books called as "Minor Prophets" – Hosea, Joel, Amos, Obadiah, Jonah, Micah, Nahum, Habakkuk, Zephaniah, Haggai, Zechariah, and Malachi.

A prophet in the Bible is a person who says "the Word of God" in 3 ways – foretelling, forth-telling, and mutual-telling. An example of (1) the foretelling discussed above, is the Word of God about 700 years before "a son named Immanuel's birth by the virgin" in Isaiah 7:14. An example of (2) forth-telling simply meaning tell forth or burst out the contents (God's words) of a bubble, is Jeremiah 23:28, "The prophet who has a dream, let him tell a dream; And he who has My word, let him speak My word faithfully. What *is* the chaff to the wheat?" says the LORD." Majority parts of the prophetic books belong to here. The last example of (3) mutual-telling, simply meaning "communication between the prophet and God," or "speak for one another," is Habakkuk 1:2, "O LORD, how long shall I cry, And You will not hear? Even cry out to You, "Violence!" And You will not save."

Now the New Testament is 27 Books, who contain 4 Gospels, 1 Acts, 21

Epistles, and 1 Revelation.

(1) The 4 Gospels are Matthew, Mark, Luke, and John. (2) 1 Acts or Apostolic History is Acts. (3) 21 Epistles or Letters are Romans, I Corinthians, II Corinthians, Galatians, Ephesians, Philippians, Colossians, I Thessalonians, II Thessalonians, I Timothy, II Timothy, Titus, Philemon – the first 13 Epistles called as "Pauline Epistles" and the last 8 Epistles called as "General Epistles" - Hebrews, James, I Peter, II Peter, I John, II John, III John, and Jude. (4) I Revelation or Apocalypse is Revelation.

Therefore, all 66 Books are "All" scripture inspired by God, the Word of God, the Whole Counsel of God, and absolutely true and absolutely authoritative. Jesus warns in Revelation 22:18-19, "For I testify to everyone who hears the words of the prophecy of this book: If anyone adds to these things, God will add to him the plagues that are written in this book; [19] and if anyone takes away from the words of the book of this prophecy, God shall take away his part from the Book of Life, from the holy city, and *from* the things which are written in this book." God says in 2 Corinthians 3:6, "who also made us sufficient as ministers of the new covenant, not of the letter but of the Spirit; for the letter kills, but the Spirit gives life." Therefore, our life is led by the Spirit in the whole counsel of God.

How can we study and/or teach the Bible by a schedule?

The schedule may be decided freely by you through prayer. Here is Henry's annual schedule to cover the Old Testament one time and the New Testament two times to be read.

A 2010 Suggested Plan for Bible Reading [xlvi]

In the spirit, to read the Bible, understand it, and apply it to each daily life

- 1/3	Ge	- 1/10	Mt
- 1/17	Ex	- 1/24	Mk
- 1/31	Lev	- 2/7	Lk
- 2/14	Nu	- 2/21	Lk
- 2/28	Dt	- 3/7	Jn
- 3/14	Jos, Jdg	- 3/21	Ac
- 3/28	Ru, I Sa	- 4/4	Ro
- 4/11	II Sa	- 4/18	I and II Co
- 4/25	I Ki	- 5/2	Gal, Eph, Php, Col
- 5/9	II Ki	- 5/16	I and II Th, I and II Ti, Tit, Phm
- 5/23	I Ch	- 5/30	Heb, Jas
- 6/6	II Ch	- 6/13	I and II Pe, I and II and III Jn, Jude
- 6/20	Ezr, Ne, Est	- 6/27	Rev
- 7/4	Job	- 7/11	Mt
- 7/18	Ps	- 7/25	Mk
- 8/1	Ps	- 8/8	Lk
- 8/15	Ps	- 8/22	Jn
- 8/29	Pr, Ecc, Ss	- 9/5	Ac
- 9/12	Isa	- 9/19	Ro
- 9/26	Isa	- 10/3	I and II Co
- 10/10	Jer	- 10/17	Gal, Eph, Php, Col

- 10/24	Jer, La	- 10/31	I and II Th, I and II Ti, Tit, Phm
- 11/7	Eze	- 11/14	Heb, Jas
- 11/21	Da	- 11/28	I and II Pe, I and II and III Jn, Jude
- 12/5	Hos, Joe, Am, Ob, Jnh, .Mic	- 12/12	Rev
- 12/19	*Topical Study	- 12/26	Na, Hab, Zep, Hag, Zec, Mal.

According to the schedule, it is suggested a guideline for the Bible study of (1) a prayer, (2) observation, (3) interpretation, (4) application, and (5) a prayer.

First, we should pray to the Lord for the Holy Spirit is teaching the Bible to us. Prayer is the communication between us and God the Father through only one mediator Jesus Christ. Prayer is seeking for His will, not pursuing our will. Prayer life is crucial for the Spirit led life to us. In the next chapter of "the Lord's Prayer," prayer is explained in detail.

As God says in 1 John 2:27 "But the anointing which you have received from Him abides in you, and you do not need that anyone teach you; but as the same anointing teaches you concerning all things, and is true, and is not a lie, and just as it has taught you, you will abide in Him," we are praying for the Holy Spirit make us understand His word.

Second, observe the studied or taught portion in the Bible. Just simply read the Bible. If you don't understand a word, you may use an English dictionary, a dictionary of the Bible, or an internet search (e.g. see http://www.Biblegateway.com/). You also may compare the studied portion of the Bible with other versions (e.g. New International Version, American Standard Version, etc).

Third, interpret yourself inspired by the Holy Spirit in context and syntax with cross-reference in the Bible. Cross-reference is a relevant verse or phrase in the Bible to your studied or taught verse. Syntax means closed verses to studied or taught verse, while context extended from the studied or taught verse to its entire chapter, up to the book. Here contextual approach is within the scope of the Bible, not with other thoughts to be merged into the Bible. But the other thoughts may be used as mere references to understand the Bible faithfully.

Syntax sometimes is so crucial for the will of God. In Philippians 2:12, God says "Therefore, my beloved, as you have always obeyed, not as in my presence only, but now much more in my absence, work out your own salvation with fear and trembling," this might be misunderstood "work out your own salvation" as "salvation with your own work" without seeing the next verse 13, "for it is God who works in you both to will and to do for *His* good pleasure." Verse 13 makes us understand "God who works," not you.

Also, context sometimes is crucial for the will of God. Satan cited Psalm 91:11-12 to tempt Jesus Christ in Matthew 4:6, "and said to Him, "If You are the Son of God, throw Yourself down. For it is written: *'He shall give His angels charge over you,'* and, *'In their hands they shall bear you up, Lest you dash your foot against a stone.'*" Seeing the entire chapter of Psalm 91, you could find its main theme "the Lord is my refuge" in verse 2 and verse 9, not to tempt the Lord.

Then, you may compare with other teaching/commentary (e.g. Wayne Kim, Chuck Smith, other biblical commentaries etc.)

Each teaching includes 3 or 4 inductive questions, weekly updated:

See http://www.calvarychapelanaheimhills.com/OnlineSermon2010.htm

See http://www.calvarychapelanaheimhills.com/OnlineSermon2009.htm

The students who went to the School of Ministry in 2000 studied the whole counsel of God for 2 years. Each lesson includes outline:

See http://www.thewordfortoday.org/?page=C2000

Fourth, learned words applicable to your life led by the Spirit may be meditated or memorized.

Jesus prays for His disciples in John 17:16-19, "They are not of the world, just as I am not of the world. [17] Sanctify them by Your truth. Your word is truth. [18] As You sent Me into the world, I also have sent them into the world. [19] And for their sakes I sanctify Myself, that they also may be sanctified by the truth." Although we are in the world, we are not of the world. Jesus wants us to be sanctified by the truth, which is the Word of God. You should think of an applied word to your particular problem for your life.

For example, if under your hard time with your employer you study the chapter 5 of Matthew, you may apply a particular verse 44, "…I say to you, love your enemies, bless those who curse you, do good to those who hate you, and pray for those who spitefully use you and persecute you," to your employer. Just meditate the verse applied to him.

Fifth, pray for closing to apply learned words to your life led by the Spirit.

If we are teachers of the Bible, we just teach all Scripture to believers faithfully or consistently. But we don't worry whether or not they are matured toward the image of Christ because that's God's work.

1.Self Questions to Confront:

(1) Why do I study the entire Bible?

(2) How many books of the Bible? What is The Old Testament? What is The New Testament?

(3) What is prophecy?

(4) What is a guideline for the Bible study? Do I use it today?

(5) What is a context or a syntax approach?

2.Verses to Meditate:

(1) Matthew 4:4, "But He answered and said, "It is written, *'Man shall not live by bread alone, but by every word that proceeds from the mouth of God.'*"

(2) Hebrews 5:12-14, "For though by this time you ought to be teachers, you need *someone* to teach you again the first principles of the oracles of God; and you have come to need milk and not solid food. [13]

For everyone who partakes *only* of milk *is* unskilled in the word of righteousness, for he is a babe. [14] But solid food belongs to those who are of full age, *that is,* those who by reason of use have their senses exercised to discern both good and evil."

(3) Isaiah 7:14," [14] Therefore the Lord Himself will give you a sign: Behold, the virgin shall conceive and bear a Son, and shall call His name Immanuel"

(4) Jeremiah 23:28," The prophet who has a dream, let him tell a dream; And he who has My word, let him speak My word faithfully. What *is* the chaff to the wheat?" says the LORD."

(5) Habakkuk 1:2, "O LORD, how long shall I cry, And You will not hear? Even cry out to You, "Violence!" And You will not save."

IV.   The Lord's Prayer

Jesus Christ taught how to pray in Matthew 6 "not to be seen of men" but to be seen "God the Father," giving the model of prayer which is "the Lord's Prayer" in Matthew 6:9-13 (KJV):

"Our Father which art in heaven, Hallowed be thy name.

[10]Thy kingdom come, Thy will be done in earth, as it is in heaven.

[11]Give us this day our daily bread.

[12]And forgive us our debts, as we forgive our debtors.

[13]And lead us not into temptation, but deliver us from evil: For thine is the kingdom, and the power, and the glory, for ever. Amen. "

To whom we pray in the Lord's Prayer is taught as to "Our Father which art in heaven." Two parts of its contents in a big picture are taught as "Worship" and "Petition."

For the 1st part, Worship God the Father is shown in the phrase of "Hallowed be thy name" and "For thine is the kingdom, and the power, and the glory, for ever. Amen." From the "worship" part can we derive "thanksgiving" in 1 Thessalonians 5:18, "in everything give thanks; for this is the will of God in Christ Jesus for you."

For the 2nd part Petition, called sometimes as "supplication" for strong petition, two kinds are taught as "petition for God" and "petition for us." For the 1st kind, (1) the petition for God is shown in the phrase "They kingdom come, Thy will be done in earth, as it is in heaven." Also in "Thy will," prayer is to seek God's will, not pursuing our will. And for the 2nd kind, (2) the petition for us is shown in the left phrases of "Give us this day our daily bread. And forgive us our debts, as we forgive our debtors."

We can divide "the petition for us" kind with "self-petition" and "petition for others or intercessions." (1) Self-petition is the petition for self in 1 John 5:14-15," Now this is the confidence that we have in Him, that if we ask anything according to His will, He hears us. [15] And if we know that He hears us, whatever we ask, we know that we have the petitions that we have asked of Him." Also It may include the self-petition for forgiveness or confession, "forgive us (above)," or in 1 John 1:9 "If we confess our sins, He is faithful and just to forgive us *our* sins and to cleanse us from all unrighteousness," (2) petition for others or intercession in Ephesians 6:18 "praying always with all prayer and supplication in the Spirit, being watchful to this end with all perseverance and supplication for all the saints" and in 1 Timothy 2:1, "Therefore I exhort first of all that supplications, prayers, intercessions, *and* giving of thanks be made for all men." Here we can point the prayer is required "in the Spirit" as well as "in faith" in James 1:6, "But let him ask in faith, with no doubting, for he who doubts is like a wave of the sea driven and tossed by the wind."

Therefore, because faith *comes* by hearing, and hearing by the Word of God (Romans 10:17), prayer to God the Father is seeking His will in Spirit and in the Word of God. This is the most valuable prayer model for our life led by the Spirit, called as "The Spirit Led Life."

1.Self Questions to Confront:

(1) What's a big picture for the Lord's prayer?

(2) Can I explain the contents of my prayer?

(3) What is the purpose of prayer? What is intercession? What is supplication?

2.Verses to Meditate:

(1) Matthew 6:9-13 (KJV), "...Our Father which art in heaven, Hallowed be thy name. [10]Thy kingdom come, Thy will be done in earth, as it is in heaven. [11]Give us this day our daily bread. [12]And forgive us our debts, as we forgive our debtors. [13]And lead us not into temptation, but deliver us from evil: For thine is the kingdom, and the power, and the glory, for ever. Amen."

(2) James 1:6, "But let him ask in faith, with no doubting, for he who doubts is like a wave of the sea driven and tossed by the wind."

(3) Ephesians 6:18, "praying always with all prayer and supplication in the Spirit, being watchful to this end with all perseverance and supplication for all the saints."

Personal Questions

Your answer to these personal questions or self questions will discover what you believe and what talents given by the Lord, able to minister to Him and His sheep for His kingdom.

A. **Please answer each question of the faith statement as to the Lord.**

1. Do you believe that the Bible to be the inspired, the only infallible, authoritative Word of God and inerrant in the original writings?

2. Do you believe that there is one God, eternally and equally existent in three persons, Father, Son, and Holy Spirit?

3. Do you believe that in the deity of our Lord Jesus Christ, in His virgin birth, in His sinless life, in His miracles, in His vicarious and atoning death through His shed blood, in His bodily resurrection, in His ascension to the right hand of the Father and in His personal return in power and glory?

4. Do you believe that in the terms of the Apostles' Creed* which are within the zone of the authoritative Word of God, as expressing fundamental facts of Christian faith?

*The Apostles' Creed

I believe in God the Father Almighty, Maker of heaven and earth, and in Jesus Christ, His only Son, our Lord:

Who was conceived by the Holy Spirit, born of the Virgin Mary, suffered under Pontius Pilate, was crucified, dead, and buried.

He descended into hell.

The third day He arose again from the dead.

He ascended into heaven and sits on the right hand of God the Father Almighty, from thence He shall come to judge the quick and the dead.

I believe in the Holy Spirit, the Holy Universal Church, the communion of saints, the forgiveness of sins, the resurrection of the body, and the life everlasting. Amen.

5. Do you believe that the lost and sinful person must be saved only through faith and person's only hope of redemption is through the shed blood of Jesus Christ, the Son of God?

6. Do you believe that in the present ministry of the Holy Spirit by whose indwelling and leading the Christian is enabled to live a Godly life?

7. Do you believe that two ordinances of both Baptism and the Lord's Supper given to the Church by Christ,

through water baptism by immersion and communion open to all believers?

8. Do you believe that in the laying hands on persons as mere methodology of prayer for acknowledgment of ordained pastors, elders, and deacons, for healing, for water baptism, for the baptism of the Holy Spirit, or for receiving gifts of the Spirit?

9. Do you believe that the Work of the Holy Spirit with gifts, fruit, leading believers, and teaching?

10. Do you believe that in the spiritual unity of believers in our Lord Jesus Christ and in "one church (*Eklesia*) on the earth," the living spiritual body, of which Christ is the Head and all regenerated persons are members?

11. Do you believe that chronologically in the rapture of the Church, Great Tribulation, Jesus' 2nd coming on earth and Judgment for beheaded Christians, Millennium Kingdom, great white throne judgment, and new heaven and earth?

B. **When you believe in the faith statement, you may apply for the following ministries at a biblical church led by the Spirit.**

God says through Peter in 1 Peter 4:10, "As each one has received a gift, minister it to one another, as good stewards of the manifold grace of God," each of us as servants of God can minister to one another with the graciously given gift in the body of Christ. Your leader is always the Holy Spirit. You are a Servant, Minister, or Steward led by the Holy Spirit, namely, "The Spirit Led Servant, Minister, or Steward."

1. **What area of your ministry inspires you? Where are you given talents?** (1) Which language - English, Farsi, Korean, Spanish, Tagalog, Chinese...etc, to understand the Whole Counsel of God, language tool is essential. We see some missionaries' ministries are very limited to such as charity ministry because of a language barrier; (2) For preaching, an Evangelist (often face to face), a Preacher (often to more people), a Missionary (often in a foreign country), (3) For Teaching, Bible Teacher (e.g. Sunday school teacher – Preschool/Kindergarten children, elementary school students, youth, college, career), Pastor, (4) Worship Team (singer, a music instrument player – guitar, piano, drum...etc).

2. **A minister/steward may serve the Lord and His sheep** at a biblical church, or any available place including a foreign country, as an employee, an independent contractor, or a volunteer, wherever our Lord leads graciously. As a matter of world law, you as a part-time or a full-time employee, an independent contractor, or a volunteer are ministering to an employer, a church. Really, we are ministering to the Lord for our life time and so we are life-time ministers everywhere (e.g., home, working place, church, or mission fields) like Jesus or Paul. Although Jesus worked as a carpenter (Mark 6:3), he was a life time minister, "the Son of Man did not come to be served, but to serve" (Matthew 20:28). Although Paul worked as a tent maker (Acts 18:3 and 1 Corinthians 9:7) not to hinder the gospel of Christ, he was a life time minister who suffered all things not to hinder the gospel of Christ (1 Corinthians 9:12). We as born-again Christians should be life-time ministers to the Lord during the Spirit Led Life in the Whole Counsel of God. A minister, a volunteer, served indigent Sheep, who were not able to support him materially. One day, he was not able to have a daily bread literally but was praying for the bread. He opened Email. A food company's manger unknown to him wanted to donate bi-weekly one bag food to a needy family. Amazingly not only he but also other 14 needy Sheep families were donated. His service was to the Lord, who took care of him and His Sheep.

3. **Please write a resume, no more than 2 pages, in this order** – 1. Name and Contact Information, 2. Your personal goal in this position, 3. Date of Birth, 4. Personal Testimony (How you became the Christian, how you discovered the Spirit was leading you into the ministry, and any evidence of that calling, e.g. Wayne Kim's Testimony above), 5. Family members (either a married or a single is fine for a minister as long as he is ordained by the Lord in Matthew 19:10-12, "His disciples said to Him, "If such is the case of the man with *his* wife, it is better not to marry." [11] But He said to them, "All cannot accept this saying, but only *those* to whom it has been given: [12] For there are eunuchs who were born thus from *their* mother's womb, and there are eunuchs who were made eunuchs by men, and there are eunuchs who have made themselves eunuchs for the kingdom of heaven's sake. He who is able to accept *it,* let him accept *it."*) 6. Career including ministries and education (Neither seminary education nor non-education is required. But the education is helpful how to understand the knowledge of God or how to serve the Lord rather than to limit God into the education frame), and 7. Two (2) References.

4. **Please note that you as an applicant and servant of the Lord should consider the following characteristics in the Bible.**

   (1)   LOVE OF CHRIST should be a compelling motive to minister to the Lord and His sheep (2 Corinthians 5:14 "For the love of Christ compels us, because we judge thus: that if One died for all, then all died").

   (2)   Such motives of personal gains (e.g., money, career, sponsor, green card....etc.) that a hireling has should be discouraged (John 10:12-15 "But a hireling, *he who is* not the shepherd, one who does not own the sheep, sees the wolf coming and leaves the sheep and flees; and the wolf catches the sheep and scatters them. [13] The hireling flees because he is a hireling and does not care about the sheep. [14] I am the good shepherd; and I know My *sheep,* and am known by My own. [15] As the Father knows Me, even so I know the Father; and I lay down My life for the sheep.")

(3) A minister/servant should be faithful to the Lord (1 Corinthians 4:1-2
"Let a man so consider us, as servants of Christ and stewards of the mysteries of God. [2] Moreover it is required in stewards that one be found faithful.").

(4) A minister/steward should be humble (Philippians 2:6-7 "who, being in the
form of God, did not consider it robbery to be equal with God, [7] but made Himself of no reputation, taking the form of a bondservant, *and* coming in the likeness of men.").

(5) A minister/steward should avoid any negative things unless they support the building up the body of Christ (e.g.,
Paul's Negative Words against Peter to build up Antioch church in Galatians 2:11-23 "[11] Now when Peter had come to Antioch, I withstood him to his face, because he was to be blamed; [12] for before certain men came from James, he would eat with the Gentiles; but when they came, he withdrew and separated himself, fearing those who were of the circumcision. [13] And the rest of the Jews also played the hypocrite with him, so that even Barnabas was carried away with their hypocrisy. [14] But when I saw that they were not straightforward about the truth of the gospel, I said to Peter before *them* all, "If you, being a Jew, live in the manner of Gentiles and not as the Jews, why do you compel Gentiles to live as Jews? [15] We *who are* Jews by nature, and not sinners of the Gentiles, [16] knowing that a man is not

justified by the works of the law but by faith in Jesus Christ, even we have believed in Christ Jesus, that we might be justified by faith in Christ and not by the works of the law; for by the works of the law no flesh shall be justified. [17] "But if, while we seek to be justified by Christ, we ourselves also are found sinners, *is* Christ therefore a minister of sin? Certainly not! [18] For if I build again those things which I destroyed, I make myself a transgressor. [19] For I through the law died to the law that I might live to God. [20] I have been crucified with Christ; it is no longer I who live, but Christ lives in me; and the *life* which I now live in the flesh I live by faith in the Son of God, who loved me and gave Himself for me. [21] I do not set aside the grace of God; for if righteousness *comes* through the law, then Christ died in vain.").

(6)   The Word of God should be understood without corruption and be practiced sincerely in the Holy Spirit (2
Corinthians 2:17 "For we are not, as so many, peddling the Word of God; but as of sincerity, but as from God, we speak in the sight of God in Christ.").

(7)   On always prayer for the Fullness of the Spirit and of the Word of God, all Christians led by the Holy Spirit will become the church led by the Spirit.
(Romans 8:14 "For as many as are led by the Spirit of God, these are sons of God")

Paul says to us in Romans 12:3-5 "For I say, through the grace given to me, to everyone who is among you, not to think *of himself* more highly than he ought to think, but to think soberly, as God has dealt to each one a measure of faith. [4] For as we have many members in one body, but all the members do not have the same function, [5] so we, *being* many, are one body in Christ, and individually members of one another."

1. Self Questions to Confront:

(1) Who is my leader during my life?

(2) What is my compelling motive to minister?

(3) Am I faithful to the Lord?

(4) Am I humble?

(5) What's controlling factor to say negative thing?

(6) Do I speak in the sight of Christ?

2. Verses to Meditate:

(1) 1 Peter 4:10, "As each one has received a gift, minister it to one another, as good stewards of the manifold grace of God."

(2) 2 Corinthians 5:14, "For the love of Christ compels us, because we judge thus: that if One died for all, then all died"

(3) 1 Corinthians 4:1-2, "Let a man so consider us, as servants of Christ and stewards of the mysteries of God. [2] Moreover it is required in stewards that one be found faithful.

(4) Philippians 2:6-7, "who, being in the form of God, did not consider it robbery to be equal with God, [7] but made Himself of no reputation, taking the form of a bondservant, *and* coming in the likeness of men."

(5) 2 Corinthians 2:17, "For we are not, as so many, peddling the Word of God; but as of sincerity, but as from God, we speak in the sight of God in Christ."

Appendix 1

Pastor Chuck Update
Mon, December 28, 2009 12:07:01 PM

From: *(Here intentionally deleted.)*

View Contact

To:

As most of you have heard, Pastor Chuck had what has been diagnosed as a "mini-stroke" early Sunday morning. Since then, he has shown continual progress and all indications are for a full and complete recovery. He is still in the hospital undergoing some tests and rehab but is showing steady improvement each day. As can be expected, he can't wait to be released and get back to the ministry here at Calvary Chapel Costa Mesa.

The hospital and family have asked that you don't call the hospital for information. Please direct inquiries to the church office at (714) 979-4422. Cards may be sent to the church office at 3800 S. Fairview Street, Santa Ana, CA, 92704 and emails may be sent to costamesa@calvarychapel.com. We will also try to keep you updated through these e-mails as new information comes in. The family appreciates the outpouring of love and support, but rather than flowers or gifts, what are most appreciated are your prayers for rest and healing.

(Here intentionally deleted here.)

Appendix 2

BYLAWS

OF

CALVARY CHAPEL OF ANAHEIM HILLS, INC.

Calvary Chapel of Anaheim Hills, Inc. has been formed as believers in the Lordship of Jesus Christ. Our supreme desire is to know Christ and be conformed into His image by the power of the Holy Spirit.

PURPOSE

The purpose of this church shall be: To win men and women to faith in Jesus Christ as Lord and Savior; to build up Christian Character "love, joy, peace, longsuffering, kindness, goodness, faithfulness, gentleness, self-control" (Gal 5:22-23); to increase Christian faithfulness "as good stewards of the manifold grace of God" (1 Pet. 4:10); to encourage individual Christians toward attaining "the measure of the stature of the fullness of Christ" (Eph. 4:13); to serve the community in every possible Christian way; to send personnel and Christian influence throughout the world by gifts and prayers for Missions.

CHARACTER, BELIEFS AND ORDINANCES

Section 1.

Calvary Chapel of Anaheim Hills, Inc., called hereinafter as church, shall not be a denominational church. It shall seek to emphasize the spiritual unity of all true believers. It shall be the policy of this church to give preeminence to the preaching of the gospel, to studying the Word of God, and to exalting the Lord Jesus Christ.

Section 2.

In order to identify the church as conservative in theology, and evangelical in spirit, we set forth this general statement of fundamental beliefs:

1. We believe the Bible to be the inspired, the only infallible, authoritative Word of God and inerrant in the original writings.
2. We believe that there is one God, eternally existent in three persons, Father, Son, and Holy Spirit.
3. We believe in the deity of our Lord Jesus Christ, in His virgin birth, in His sinless life, in His miracles, in His vicarious and atoning death through His shed blood, in His bodily resurrection, in His ascension to the right hand of the Father and in His personal return in power and glory.
4. We believe that the lost and sinful man must be saved, and that man's only hope of redemption is through the shed blood of Jesus Christ, the Son of God.
5. We believe in the present ministry of the Holy Spirit by whose indwelling the Christian is enabled to live a Godly life.
6. We believe in the resurrection of both the saved and the unsaved; they that are saved unto the resurrection of life and they that are unsaved unto the resurrection of damnation.
7. We believe in the spiritual unity of believers in our Lord Jesus Christ.

Section 3.

The church will observe regularly the two New Testament ordinances of water baptism and the Lord's Supper. These ordinances are observed in obedience to our Lord Jesus Christ, as Acts of love and devotion, and are not considered to be necessary for our salvation.

SOVEREIGNTY AND FELLOWSHIP OF THE LOCAL CHURCH
Section 1.

Believing in the independence of the local church with full freedom of deliberation, decision, and deportment under God without restriction, supervision or domination from any outside individual, organization, or institution, this church is to be completely autonomous and self-governing and will not affiliate with any organization which seeks to exercise control over the local church. However, this Church may join in the Calvary Chapel Outreaching Fellowships at the Calvary Chapel of Costa Mesa, California.

Section 2.

This church desires the fellowship of all evangelical churches and Christian groups and will cooperate with them to promote the cause of Jesus Christ.

MEMBERSHIP
Section 1.

To qualify for membership in this church, applicants must have received Jesus Christ as their personal Savior, shall subscribe to the said Statement of Fundamental Beliefs upon being approved by pastor and church board – it is desirable for members to sign the church register.

Section 2.

The membership of this Church shall have three classifications: active roll, inactive roll, and non-resident roll.

A. Upon application for membership approved by the Pastor and the Church Board and the admittance of a member   at any regular service, a person shall be entered on the active roll of the Church and shall be deemed an active member until the membership classification is changed as provided in this MEMBERSHIP;
B. Any member who has been absent from the Church for an unreasonable period of time without manifesting an interest in said Church, shall be placed on the inactive roll upon the recommendation of the Church Board. However, mere sickness, age or other disability shall not of itself be sufficient for transfer to the inactive roll;
C. Any member who temporarily resides in another locality for a period of one hundred twenty days or more, or members who are in another locality because of being in the Armed Forces, Missionary work or other Christian service, shall be placed on the non-resident roll.

GOVERNMENT

Section 1.

A. The government of the church shall be founded upon the lordship and direction of Jesus Christ. Everyone in authority at the church continually seeks His mind and will, through His Spirit and the Word of God in all actions and decisions.
B. The Board of Directors, who is elders, shall serve under the leadership and direction of the Pastor.   Also elders and deacons shall minister to the church in various capacities under the direction of the Pastor.

C. The governing Board of the Church shall be known as the Board of Directors, consisting of the Pastor and at least two (2) other members, but no more than eight (8) other members, elected by the members on the active roll. The total numbers of the Board members must be 3, 5, 7, or 9.

Section 2.

The Church Board shall be the governing body of the Church and shall conduct the transaction of the Church, except that it shall not be able to encumber, transfer, sell or purchase any real property without the approval of a majority of the members on the active roll of the Church consenting to such action at a membership meeting called for that purpose.

Section 3.

A majority vote of a majority of Board members present (called as "a majority of the Board"), shall as a matter of law constitute a quorum for any action unless a higher percentage is required elsewhere in the Bylaws. However, biblically the unanimous vote of all Board members present shall be preferred for one and same God's direction through prayer.

Section 4.

Regular meetings of the Church Board shall be held in each calendar month at a time and place to be determined by a majority of the Board. Special meeting may be called by the Pastor or any two (2) members of the Church Board. Any meeting may be held by conference telephone or similar communication equipment.

Section 5.

Any member of the Church Board, who is removed from the active roll, shall automatically be removed from the Church Board. If any Board member misses two or more regular meetings during a calendar year, he may be removed by two-thirds of the remaining Church Board members. However, he may issue a power of attorney to an active member to do a specified duty during a specified period because of sickness, other disability, or other valid reasons, upon the unanimous approval of the Board.

Section 6.

The Church Board members except the Pastor shall be elected at an annual meeting of the active membership of the Church. Three members of the Board shall be elected to serve a three (3) year term at the annual membership meeting. No board member shall succeed himself in office who has served full three year term unless a qualified elder (stated below) is unavailable.

Section 7.

Vacancies on the Church Board members during the calendar year shall be filled by vote of the majority of the remaining Directors in office. A successor director so elected shall serve for the unexpired term of his predecessor.

Section 8.

All elections by members on the active roll may be determined by secret ballot.

Section 9.

The Church Board shall serve as a nominating committee.

DUTIES OF DIRECTORS OF THE CHURCH BOARD

Section 1.

The directors of the Church Board shall be the Pastor and the duly elected Directors.

Section 2.   Duties of the Pastor
A. The Pastor shall be an ordained minister of good reputation, conservative in theology and willing to serve an undenominational church without attempting to promote any denominational interest.
B. The Pastor shall have the general supervision of the entire ministries of the Church and shall perform all necessary duties relating to such supervision. The Pastor shall have charge of all Church services.

Section 3. Duties of the President of the Corporation:
A. The Pastor shall be a member of the Church Board and shall be the President of the Board.
B. The President shall preside at all Church Board meetings and meetings of Church membership; the President shall appoint a parliamentarian who shall assist him at the general Church meeting.

Section 4. Duties of the Secretary

220

The Secretary shall keep an accurate record of the procedure and decisions of all meetings, attend to the correspondence of the church, and perform any other necessary duties as the Church directs. The Secretary shall keep an accurate record of the Church Membership rolls.

Section 5. Duties of Treasurer

The Treasurer shall be responsible for all monies coming into the church and shall make disbursements in accordance with the annual budget and the special decisions of the church. He shall keep itemized accounts of all income and disbursements and render written statements of same at each regular meeting of the church. The book of accounts shall be closed at the end of each calendar year and a comprehensive report of income and disbursement shall be represented.

AUXILIARIES

A support group, multi-cultural group, study group, or any other organization, whose memberships are primarily for a church activity, shall be considered an auxiliary of the church and shall be subject to bylaws of the church. An auxiliary organization shall exist only in cooperation with the official church board.

Calvary Chapel Anaheim Hills Press or CCAH Press is an auxiliary of the church in terms of "Copyright, loyalty, any other intellectual property, and/or any other's net profit of the book/Tape/CD/DVD/MP3 published by "CCAH Press" belonged in pro rata to 70 % for CCAH and to 30 % for an Author and Employee in CCAH respectively, while by any other publisher(s) than CCAH Press, to 30% for CCAH and to 70% for him or her. Non-employee such as volunteer or independent contractor is not subject to this clause. CCAH reserves the right to deny and/or accept him or her to publish through the CCAH Press either with or without conditions."

"Asaph Missions" team is an auxiliary of Calvary Chapel Anaheim Hills, having two parts to abide in the true Vine Christ (1) to open up wider a supply channel of materials and resources to teach the Bible to people in USA, N./S. Korea, Muslim countries, Kenya, China, Mexico, Europe, and over the world and so locals can have assistance in establishing churches as the Holy Spirit leads and the Whole Counsel of God to feed hungry souls and to invite whoever is interested in missions for annual Mission trips in China and in Mexico and annual world mission retreat and fellowship in USA and (2) to make a transnational discipleship team to be witnesses to Christ in USA, N./S. Korea, Muslim countries, Kenya, China, Mexico, Europe, and over the world for strengthening and vision inspiration.

MEETINGS

Section 1.

The church shall hold the following meetings: annual meetings, held on the fourth week in December and special meetings.

Section 2.

Special meetings may be called by the Pastor or the President of the Corporation following any regular meeting of the church or at any other convenient time. When the agenda at hand concerns the buying or selling of church real property or the filing of an elective office, announcement of such meeting shall be made for two Sundays prior to the date of the meeting.

Section 3.

No transaction shall be conducted without a quorum consisting of ten percent (10%) of the voting membership of the church. A majority vote of the members present shall be required to transact all actions except as stated elsewhere in this Bylaw.

MINISTERIAL RELATIONS

Section 1.   Elders

A. According to 1 Timothy 3:1-7 and Titus 1:5-9, an elder shall be a man of high moral character, a one-woman man, temperate, prudent, respectable, not self-willed, self-controlled, just, devote, and not covetous.

B. An elder shall be a man who rules his home well and whose children follow his example.

C. An elder shall be a man who handles himself uprightly among others, who is not a drunkard, not a striker, but rater, gentle, uncontentious, hospitable, a lover of good, and one of good reputation in the world.

D. An elder shall be a mature believer who is apt and able to teach.

E. The number of Elders shall be left to the discretion of the Pastor according to the needs of the congregation but the number is no more than twenty (20).   After the Board members' praying for God's direction during at least one week, each Director, independently and without talking each other, shall submit a secret ballot and written recommendation to the President of the Board at the Board meeting.   Then, the President shall ratify only unanimous recommendation for a qualified elder with the direction of only one and same God. The ratified elders may be ministering for a lifetime unless disqualified biblically or resign.

F. Elders may serve as Directors of the Board and/or Officers of this Church. The Directors shall receive no compensation for their services but can be allowed reimbursement for reasonable expenses incurred in the carrying out of their service to this church. The Officers may be compensated. The Officers, who are daily working at this Church, shall be the Pastor and may be Pastoral Assistants.

Section 2. Serving Pastor

A. The Serving Pastor shall minister unto the Lord in regular personal worship and praise. He shall give himself to the ministry of the Word of God and prayer (Acts 6:4) and seek to walk uprightly before the Lord in his personal life. He shall continually seek God's will to guide him in all his actions and decisions. The Pastor shall be the teaching His sheep. He shall give considerable time to study of the Word and shall teach the Bible to His sheep by precept and example. He shall feed them, equip them for the work of the ministry, and guard the church against the attack of the enemy.

B. The Pastor shall be a member of the Church Board and shall be the President of said Board. He shall oversee the transaction of the church on a daily basis and give leadership direction to the Pastoral Assistants, the Board of Directors members, and elders, and deacons, as well as the other church body and its various ministries. The Pastor shall have general supervision of the entire church and be in authority or charge of all services, gathering, and meetings.

C. The Pastor shall be qualified according to the said 1 Timothy 3:1-7and Titus 1:5-9, as well as Ephesians 4:11-12, being a Spirit gifted teacher of the Word of God, an ordained pastor of good reputation, Biblically conservative in theology, Christ centered and Spirit-filled.

D. The Pastor's initial salary shall be specified at the time of his calling. The church shall as able make provision for an adequate compensation for the Pastor. The Pastor shall be entitled to an annual vacation of two weeks. The church shall also defray the costs of sending the Pastor to out of town conferences and conventions for the church as approved by the Board.

Section 3. Deacons

A. According to 1 Timothy 3:8-13, a deacon is serious, not double tongued, not a drunkard, one-woman man, obedient to the faith, and mature.

B. Deacons shall carry on various ministries within His body to meet the physical needs of the church under the direction and encouragement of the Pastor, pastoral staff, and elders.

C. Deacons shall counsel with the Pastor, pastoral staff and elders regarding the physical needs which arise in the body; they shall pray for any of the flock for whom they are caring; they shall serve the flock for exercising hospitality, love, care, and good counsel.

D. The number of Deacons shall be left to the discretion of the Pastor according to the needs of the congregation. With counsel of the Board of Directors the Pastor may appoint Deacons for a lifetime and may review each appointment yearly.

Section 4.

A. A minister may be asked to resign for Biblical cause (i.e. the practicing of sin, attested to by two or more witnesses, according to the Word of God). A minister, other than the Pastor, may be removed by a majority of the Board, but the said unanimous vote of all Board members present is preferred through prayer. The Pastor may be removed by a three-fourths vote of the Elders and Deacons presently serving at the church at that time, and then by a two-thirds vote of a majority of the active members present. Vote shall be by secret ballot. A thirty day notice shall be given to the removed Pastor or financial remuneration for that period of time shall be paid to him.

B. In the event of a vacancy in the pastorate, the Board of Directors may seek a new Pastor. The retiring or resigning Pastor may nominate a successor with a majority of the Board and/or participate in the selection of his successor. In the selection process, the Board shall serve as a Pulpit Committee to seek a suitable candidate for Pastor. After presenting to the church a candidate for Pastor, the Pulpit Committee shall, if they are agreed that the candidate is acceptable, recommend the candidate to the church. Action on the Pulpit Committee's recommendation shall be taken at a special meeting called for this purpose. If the candidate receive a two thirds vote of the majority of the active members present he shall be considered elected. Vote shall be by secret ballot. Any valid and qualified absentee ballots will be valid if they are on hand at the time of the meeting.

C. Pastoral Assistants shall be born-again Christians. The Pastoral Assistants such as Assistant or Associate Pastors, Directors of Christian Education, Youth Ministers, Music Ministers, Visitation Ministers, Clerical Ministers and any other assistants deemed necessary by agreement between the Pastor and the Board shall be recommended by the Board to the church. It shall be the prerogative of the Pastor, after counseling with the Board, to ask for the resignation of Pastoral assistant if they are not in harmony with the total church program as directed by the Pastor.

D. Should any disputes develop in, from, with, or to the Church, the board shall resolve them according to Matthew 18:15-17. But they not resolved shall be subject to a Christian mediation and arbitration process (e.g. peace maker ministries, Christian Legal Aid, etc.), according to 1 Corinthians 6:6, rather than an earthly Court. Should a minister, who holds an office of a deacon/deaconess, an elder, or a pastor, on the active or non-residence roll in the membership, place it voluntarily or involuntarily on the inactive roll, his or her office shall be automatically terminated in, from, with, or to the Church unless the Board makes a different opinion according to Revelation 3:10. Should the minister have a conflict of ministry schedule in, from, with, or to the church, he or she shall be highly recommended to minister to the least sheep according to Matthew 25:40, by the Board.

FISCAL MATTERS

Section 1.

The fiscal year of the church shall be from January 1st to December 31st.

Section 2.

The necessary finances for conducting the regular activities of the church will be obtained through a system of tithes, thanksgiving offering, willing offering, gifts, and regular offerings. Gifts designated for special purposes will be indicated for the specific purpose. All compensation and reimbursement shall not exceed fifty percent (50%) of the all revenues at this Church.

PROPERTY RIGHTS

Section 1.

The title to all real property of the corporation shall be in the name of the corporation and no member or group of members shall have any individual property rights in the assets of the corporation.

Section 2.

In the event that the corporation is dissolved, the properties shall be sold and all proceeds, above liabilities, proportioned on the basis of current support, shall be divided among the missions receiving support from the church.

RITES OF ORDINATION

Section 1.

Only our Sovereign Holy God can truly call and ordain His children for service in the ministry of the Gospel of Jesus Christ. The calling of a minister is not the result of a title, rather the title is a result of his calling. The calling is recognized as from the one and only true and living God. It is man's privilege and specifically the privilege of the overseers of the true church of Jesus Christ, to ratify the ordination of God when such is obviously placed upon a man's life. The purpose of this Article is to provide for the ordination rites of ministers of the Gospel of Jesus Christ.

Section 2.

A candidate for Ordination must qualify under all of the following:

A. A candidate for ordination must be a "born again" believer in Jesus Christ as described by our Lord in the third chapter of the Gospel of John.

B. A candidate must believe that there is only one God, eternally existent in three persons: God the Father, God the Son, and God the Holy Spirit.

C. A candidate must meet the scriptural requirements for the office of an Elder as described in the Bible, references 1 Timothy 3:1-7 and Titus 1:5-9.

D. A candidate must believe and render evidence of his belief that the Bible is the complete and divinely inspired Word of God and that God has not added, deleted, or altered this work with subsequent writings or revelations and uphold God's Word as the only measuring rod by which we should conduct our lives.

E. A candidate must have completed at least four (4) years of Bible Study, with at least two (2) years concentrated study under a known, approved Bible teacher.

F. A candidate must believe in the objectives of this body and its concepts concerning the gifts and work of the Holy Spirit today.

G. A candidate should have evidenced the obvious calling of God on his life in terms of ministerial experience and report.

Section 3.

A. Each person fulfilling the above qualifications, and upon their proper presentation tot the Board of Directors of this body, will receive full consideration for ordination into the ministry of the Gospel of Jesus Christ.

B. Upon unanimous approval of all Board members present, the candidate will be ordained as a minister of the Gospel of Jesus Christ with the right to perform ministerial functions, in accordance with the laws of the land and the ordinances of God's Holy Word with all prerogatives of such a calling and office.

C. All candidates, successful or otherwise, will be notified by the Board of Directors as to their decision in writing within two weeks of the Board's final action or decision.

Section 4.

The following is the text of the Certificate of Ordination to be issued to each successful candidate:

This is to certify that Pastor _____ was duly ordained by _____ as a minister of the Gospel of Jesus Christ. He has completed all studies and has met all of the requirements of this body for recognition of such office. Further by the rite of ordination this date he is duly ordained to perform all ministerial functions without limit as accorded by the laws of the land in compliance with the ordinances of God's Holy Church as set forth in the Holy Bible. We now pray for God's divine blessing and the power of the Holy Spirit upon him

Given this _____ day of _____, 200_____

_____

Director

_____

Director

_____

Director (Treasurer)

_____

Director (Secretary)

_____

Director   (President)

(Corporate Seal)

AMENDMENTS

Section 1.

The bylaws may be amended, modified or rescinded by a two-thirds (2/3) majority vote of the qualified active members present at any regular or special meeting for transaction provided that due notice is given that such action is to be introduced at such meeting. For purposes of this article, due notice shall consist of no less than public announcement for two Sundays and the posting of the proposed amendment in a conspicuous place at least one week prior to said meeting.

Section 2.

Proposed amendments to these bylaws shall be made by the Board and approved by a majority vote of the church at a regular meeting.

MISCELLANEOUS

Section 1.   Execution of Documents

The Board may authorize any officer or officers, agent or agents, to enter into any contract or execute any instrument in the name of and on behalf of the church. Such authority may be generally or confined to specific instances.   Unless so authorized by the board, no officer, agent or other person shall have any power or authority to bind the church by any contract or engagement or to pledge its credit or to render it liable for any purpose or to any amount.

Section 2.   Inspection of Bylaws

The church shall keep in its principal officer the original or a copy of this bylaws, as amended or otherwise altered to date, certified by the Secretary, which shall be open to inspection by the members at all reasonable times during the office hours.

Section 3.   Construction and Definitions

Unless the context otherwise requires, the general provision, rules of construction and definitions contained in the California General Nonprofit Corporation Law shall govern the construction of these bylaws.

CERTIFICATE

We, the undersigned, do hereby certify:

1. That we are the duly elected Directors of   CALVARY CHAPEL OF ANAHEIM HILLS, INC, a California Non-Profit Religious Corporation.

2. That the foregoing bylaws, consisting of 8 pages, constitute the Bylaws of said corporation on.........................   (...*intentionally deleted here.....*)

IN WITNESS WHEREOF, we have executed this Certificate this..... day of........, at Anaheim Hills, California.

(All directors' names intentionally deleted...)

_____
Director

_____
Director

_____
Director (Treasurer)

_____
Director (Secretary)

_____
Director   (President)

(Corporate Seal)

Endnotes

[i] Charles Colson, "The Body," (Texas: Word Publishing, 1992).

[ii] Carl Westerland, "Spiritual Formation," (California: Calvary Chapel of Costa Mesa School of Ministry, 1997).

[iii] Chuck Smith, "Living Water," (California: The Word For Today, 2007).

[iv] Chuck Smith, "Why Grace Changes Everything?" (California: The Word For Today, 2007).

[v] Chuck Smith, "The Tribulation and the Church," (California: The Word For Today, 1980).

[vi] George Bryson, "Five Points of Calvinism," (California: The Word For Today, 1996).

[vii] Chuck Smith, "Calvinism, Arminianism and the Word of God: A Calvary Chapel Perspective," Found at http://Biblefacts.org/church/CalvinismVsArminianism%20.pdf

[viii] Carl Westurlund's lecture in a class, 1999.

[ix] Bob Hoekstra, "The Psychologizing of the Faith," (California: The Word For Today, 1994).

[x] Chuck Smith, "Calvary Chapel Distincitves," (California: The Word For Today, 2000).

[xi] L. E. Romaine, "Second," (California: The Word For Today, 1996).

[xii] Howard G. Hendricks and William D. Hendricks, "As Iron Sharpens Iron," (Illinois: Moody Press, 1995).

[xiii] "A Venture in Faith," Video (California: Logos Media, 2007).

[xiv] Chuck Smith, "How and Why Series," Video (California: The Word For Today, 2005).

[xv] Hank Hanegraaff, "Christianity in Crisis," (Tennessee: Thomas Nelson, 2009).

[xvi] Ibid.

[xvii] James A. Berley, "Holy Laughter and the Toronto Blessing," (Michigan: Zondervan Publishing House, 1995).

[xviii] Michael L Brown, "Whatever Happened to the Power of God," (Pennsylvania: Destiny Image, 1991).

[xix] See http://en.wikipedia.org/wiki/Living_Stream_Ministry;

[xx] See http://en.wikipedia.org/wiki/Watchman_Nee

[xxi] Watchman Nee, "The Normal Christian Life," (Illinois: Tyndale House Publishers, Inc, 1977).

[xxii] Henry H. Halley, "Halley's Bible Handbook," (Michigan: Zondervan, 1965).

[xxiii] See http://en.wikipedia.org/wiki/Seventh-day_Adventist

[xxiv] See http://en.wikipedia.org/wiki/Emerging_church

[xxv] See http://en.wikipedia.org/wiki/Messianic_Judaism

[xxvi] Henry H. Halley, (ibid.).

[xxvii] See http://www.allaboutcreation.org/evolution-vs-creation.htm

[xxviii] John MacArthur, "The Battle for the Beginning," (California: W Publishing, 2001).

[xxix] See http://en.wikipedia.org/wiki/New_Age

[xxx] See http://en.wikipedia.org/wiki/Atheism

[xxxi] John F. MacArthur, Jr., "Why Believe the Bible," (California: Regal Book, 1980).

[xxxii] John McDowell and Don Stewart, "Reasons," (Illinois: Tyndale House, 1981).

[xxxiii] John F MacArthur, Jr. "Focus on Fact," (New Jersey: Fleming H.

Revell, 1977).

[xxxiv] Charles H Campbell, "Answers Skeptics," (California: Aquintas, 2005).

[xxxv] See http://en.wikipedia.org/wiki/Galaxy

[xxxvi] Ainslie Thomas Embree, Stephen N. Hay, William Theodore De Bary, "Sources of Indian Tradition: Modern India and Pakistan," (New York: Columbia University Press, 1988). Found at http://en.wikipedia.org/wiki/Dharma

[xxxvii] Hiro G. Badlani, "Hinduism: Path of the Ancient Wisdom," 2008. Found at http://en.wikipedia.org/wiki/Dharma

[xxxviii] See http://www.hindunet.org/vedas/

[xxxix] See http://en.wikipedia.org/wiki/Confucianism

[xl] The Holy Qur'an, Arabic Text and English Translation, (Delaware: Noor Foundation International Inc., 2003).

[xli] See http://www.answers.com/topic/talmud

[xlii] Henry H. Halley, (ibid.).

[xliii] See http://en.wikipedia.org/wiki/Church_of_Christ,_Scientist

[xliv] The Office of Alternate Education, "Compendium of Pastoral Theology," Volume 1 (Colorado: The Christian and Missionary Alliance, 1990).

[xlv] Ibid.

[xlvi] Henry H. Halley, (ibid.).

238

INDEX

Abomination of Desolation, 92

Agape, 30, 33, 37, 45, 70, 71, 93, 148, 155, 161, 165, 171

Ancestor worship, 158, 160, 172

Apocalypse, 195

Apocrypha, 158, 170, 173, 181

Apostles' Creed, 15, 24, 205,

Apostolic History, 195

Archaeology, 164, 166

Arminianism, 97,100,101

Asaph Missions, 222

Atheism, 160

Baby Dedication, 141, 144, 146, 147

Balance, 29, 108, 115, 116, 134, 136, 165

Baptism with the Holy Spirit, 68, 75, 111

Booby Traps, 68, 85

Buddhism, 8-10, 16, 160, 171

Building, 18, 111, 116, 119, 132, 135, 139, 210

Calvinism, 12, 13, 94, 97, 100, 101, 112

Carnal Judgment, 45-46

Casting Down, 45

Catholicism, 158

Centrality, 112

Christian, 25-31, 131, 146, 151, 153, 154, 155

Christianity, 10, 16, 30, 31, 109, 152, 154, 157, 160, 177

Christian's Devil Possession, 16, 149

Christmas, 177

Church Dedication, 73, 75, 141

Church Government, 110

Church of Christ, Scientist, 20, 168, 174

Communion Service, 14, 141, 142-147, 168

Compromise, 13, 52, 102, 106, 156, 157, 158, 160, 161

Concurrent Condition, 98, 100, 102

Conform, 12, 27, 47, 55, 69, 75, 119, 139, 151, 161, 166, 214

Confucianism, 8, 9, 153, 158, 160, 172

Context, 127, 132, 137, 153, 157, 198, 200, 233

Conversion, 68, 69, 111, 154

Cult, 43

Deity, 49, 161, 184, 190, 205, 215

Dharma, 8, 9, 170, 171, 181

Direction, 26, 33, 52, 53, 54, 73, 75, 102, 103, 104, 120, 121, 122, 132, 133, 217, 218, 223, 225

Discerning, 55, 62, 72, 152, 163, 187, 191

Distinctives, 108

Divine Kingdom Seeker, 117

Dwell, 30, 68, 88, 92, 111, 167, 177, 179, 186, 206, 215

Easter, 8, 12, 14, 178

Emerging Church, 15, 156, 162

Empower, 29, 52, 109, 111, 126, 155

Epistles, 148, 195

Eros, 30

Evangelist, 20, 33, 42, 61, 64, 74, 116, 132, 208

Evolutionism, 158, 160

Evolutional Creation, 13, 160, 162

Exhorter, 65

Faith, 28, 59

Faithful, 60, 66, 70, 71, 76, 83, 92, 104, 210

Feeling Good Doctrine, 151

Finance, 127, 135, 137, 228

First Resurrection, 189

Flexibility, 135

Free Will, 99

Fruit of the Spirit, 70, 76, 85, 187, 190

Garden, 80, 85, 99

Gifts of the Spirit, 55, 57, 187, 207

Gospel, 11, 13, 14, 16, 19, 31, 33, 43, 194, 208, 210, 214, 229, 230

Grace, 10, 18, 36, 48, 54, 64, 76-87

Great Commandments, 31

Great Tribulation, 52, 88, 89, 90, 92, 93, 113, 189, 207

Great White Throne Judgment, 189

Growing Faith, 59

Guideline for Preaching, 33

Guideline for the Bible Study, 197

Guideline to give, 66

Healing Faith, 59

Heretic, 43

Hindu, 160, 170, 171, 172, 181

Hippie Movement, 132

Historical Books, 193

Holy Spirit, 22, 28, 48-54

Inductive, 112,137, 193, 199

Institutionalization, 139

Irresistible Grace, 96

Ivy Tower, 135, 139

Jehovah's Witness, 20, 168, 176, 177

Justice, 67, 138

Koran, 172

Limited Atonement, 95

Living Theology, 134

Living Water, 47, 70

Logos, 18, 28, 168

Mammon Seeker, 117, 119

Marriage, 58, 131, 143, 144, 175

McChurch, 19, 109, 117, 119

Means, 119, 129

Memorial Service, 141, 142, 143, 145, 146

Mentor, 20, 130

Mercy, 67, 138, 151, 172

Messianic Jews, 157

Millennial Kingdom, 92

Minister, 104, 108, 109, 112, 114, 123, 132, 205

Miracle, 8, 49, 55, 60, 61

Monotheist, 26, 27

Mormon, 168, 170, 174, 175

Moses' Seat, 73, 74

Natural Man, 71, 179

New Age, 15, 160

New Covenant, 114, 123, 147, 160, 195,

New Wave of the Holy Spirit, 152

Object, 119, 230

Obstructable Grace, 100

Offerings, 117, 119, 137, 141, 228

Old Testament, 124, 138, 155, 173, 193

Openness, 134-135

Parable, 33, 34, 148, 161, 171, 173, 178

Par-nirvana, 8, 171

Pentateuch, 194

Perseverance of the Saints, 96

Philia, 30

Postmodernism, 14, 156

Positive Thought Doctrine, 151

Preaching, 33, 208

Preaching Guideline, 33

Pre-Millennium, 93, 190

Pre-Tribulation, 190

Priority, 94, 112, 136

Promises to Abraham, 79, 81

Prophecy, 134, 152, 163, 164, 166, 194

Prophetic Books, 193, 194

Prosperity Gospel, 11, 150

Psychologizing, 102

Purify, 52

Rapture, 89, 91, 93, 113, 188, 190, 207

Regeneration, 68, 75, 95

Rema, 28

Responsibility, 66, 84, 127

Restraints, 90

Resurrection, 14, 15, 31, 39, 40, 91, 93, 145, 156, 175, 184, 215

Royalty, 84

Salt & Light, 29

Saving Faith, 59

Second, 92, 124

Second Resurrection, 91, 93, 189

Self Led Life, 17, 26

Serving Pastor, 74, 224

Seventh-Day Adventists, 155

Seventy Weeks, 89

Single, 209

Spirit Led Life, 17, 20, 24, 27, 85, 149, 155, 197, 203, 208

Spiritual Discernment, 45, 46

Spiritual Law, 65

Steward, 84, 207, 210

Storge, 30

Sufficiency, 104, 114, 118

Supremacy, 114

Syntax, 198

Talmud, 173

Teaching, 33

Theocracy, 66, 110, 116

Three G, 139

Tithes, 66, 138, 228

Tongues, 15, 55, 63, 68, 70, 152, 163, 187

Toronto Blessing, 152

Total Depravity, 95, 97, 98

Trinity, 49, 155, 172

Unconditional Election, 12, 95, 98, 100

Unity, 133, 154, 155, 188, 207, 214, 215

Universal Atonement, 12, 100

Vedas, 172

Venture in Faith, 115, 131, 136, 139, 150

Watchman Nee, 153

Whole Counsel of God, 20, 73, 112, 193, 208, 222

Witness Lee, 153

Witness to Jesus, 29, 31, 135, 189, 222

Word Faith Movement, 149

Work of the Holy Spirit, 52, 74, 105, 108, 111, 116, 131, 134, 136, 156, 187, 207, 230

Last Verses To Meditate

(John 3:16) "For God so loved the world that He gave His only begotten Son, that whoever believes in Him should not perish but have everlasting life."

(Acts 1:8) "But you shall receive power when the Holy Spirit has come upon you; and you shall be witnesses to Me in Jerusalem, and in all Judea and Samaria, and to the end of the earth."

(Romans 8:14) "For as many as are led by the Spirit of God, these are sons of God."

(Acts 20:27) "For I have not shunned to declare to you the whole counsel of God."

(2 Corinthians 10:5) "casting down arguments and every high thing that exalts itself against the knowledge of God, bringing every thought into captivity to the obedience of Christ,"

(Mark 12:30-31)*"And you shall love the LORD your God with all your heart, with all your soul, with all your mind, and with all your strength.'* This *is* the first commandment. [31] And the second, like *it, is* this: *'You shall love your neighbor as yourself.'* There is no other commandment greater than these."

(Matthew 28:18-20) "And Jesus came and spoke to them, saying, "All authority has been given to Me in heaven and on earth. [19] Go therefore and make disciples of all the nations, baptizing them in the name of the Father and of the Son and of the Holy Spirit, [20] teaching them to observe all things that I have commanded you; and lo, I am with you always, *even* to the end of the age." Amen."

(Luke 15:7) "I say to you that likewise there will be more joy in heaven over one sinner who repents than over ninety-nine just persons who need no repentance."

You may present a freewill offering to the Lord for the Asaph Missions team (e.g. N Korea, Muslim countries...), sending it to CCAH, PO Box 27693, Anaheim Hills, CA 92809, U.S.A.

Dr Wayne Kim is a Pastor and Teacher of Calvary Chapel Anaheim Hills in Anaheim Hills, California. He was born in spirit of Buddhism, mixed with Confucianism, and grew up in the fear of death until youth. After becoming a born again Christian, he faced turmoil of denominations, evolutionism, postmodernism, the word of faith, prosperity gospel, and other thoughts, etc, resulting in his emptiness and his thirst for truth. While he was a college teacher and Sunday School the Bible teacher, his deeper thirst for the Word of God led him to go to study theology and the Bible at the School of Ministry at Calvary Chapel Costa Mesa, where he has been taught, influenced, and mentored by Pastors Carl Westurlund, Chuck Smith, and Duke Kim. Chuck impacted on him to have an answer his life time thirst to be filled in the balance between the teaching of the Whole Counsel of God and an open heart to the work of the Holy Spirit. After being called a pastor, he has met people and preached Gospel and taught the Bible, thinking of every thought how to be subject to the knowledge of God. Throughout his taught thoughts and experiences, how our Lord is leading our life in the Whole Counsel of God is spiritually, biblically, empirically, and practically discussed. To anyone who wants to be the Spirit Led Life, the Spirit Led Minister, and the Spirit Led Church, this book would be helpful and profitable in the Whole Counsel of God.

Source of the Cover Photo: www.sxc.hu

Order of the Book: Amazon.com